CAMBRIDGE
UNIVERSITY PRESS

Physics
for Cambridge IGCSE™

WORKBOOK

David Sang & Darrell Hamilton

CAMBRIDGE
UNIVERSITY PRESS

Shaftesbury Road, Cambridge CB2 8EA, United Kingdom

One Liberty Plaza, 20th Floor, New York, NY 10006, USA

477 Williamstown Road, Port Melbourne, VIC 3207, Australia

314–321, 3rd Floor, Plot 3, Splendor Forum, Jasola District Centre, New Delhi – 110025, India

103 Penang Road, #05-06/07, Visioncrest Commercial, Singapore 238467

Cambridge University Press is part of the University of Cambridge.

It furthers the University's mission by disseminating knowledge in the pursuit of education, learning and research at the highest international levels of excellence.

www.cambridge.org
Information on this title: www.cambridge.org/9781108744515

© Cambridge University Press & Assessment 2021

First edition 2010
Second edition 2014
Third edition 2021

20 19 18 17 16 15 14 13 12 11 10 9 8 7

Printed in the Netherlands by Wilco BV

A catalogue record for this publication is available from the British Library

ISBN 978-1-108-74451-5 Paperback

Additional resources for this publication at www.cambridge.org/go

DEDICATED TEACHER AWARDS

Teachers play an important part in shaping futures. Our Dedicated Teacher Awards recognise the hard work that teachers put in every day.

Thank you to everyone who nominated this year; we have been inspired and moved by all of your stories. Well done to all of our nominees for your dedication to learning and for inspiring the next generation of thinkers, leaders and innovators.

Congratulations to our incredible winner and finalists!

WINNER

Patricia Abril
New Cambridge School, Colombia

Stanley Manaay
Salvacion National High School, Philippines

Tiffany Cavanagh
Trident College Solwezi, Zambia

Helen Comerford
Lumen Christi Catholic College, Australia

John Nicko Coyoca
University of San Jose-Recoletos, Philippines

Meera Rangarajan
RBK International Academy, India

For more information about our dedicated teachers and their stories, go to
dedicatedteacher.cambridge.org

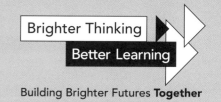

Brighter Thinking
Better Learning
Building Brighter Futures Together

› Contents

> How to use this series

We offer a comprehensive, flexible array of resources for the Cambridge IGCSE™ Physics syllabus. We provide targeted support and practice for the specific challenges we've heard that learners face: learning science with English as a second language; learners who find the mathematical content within science difficult; and developing practical skills.

The coursebook provides coverage of the full Cambridge IGCSE Physics syllabus. Each chapter explains facts and concepts, and uses relevant real-world examples of scientific principles to bring the subject to life. Together with a focus on practical work and plenty of active learning opportunities, the coursebook prepares learners for all aspects of their scientific study. At the end of each chapter, examination-style questions offer practice opportunities for learners to apply their learning.

The digital teacher's resource contains detailed guidance for all topics of the syllabus, including common misconceptions identifying areas where learners might need extra support, as well as an engaging bank of lesson ideas for each syllabus topic. Differentiation is emphasised with advice for identification of different learner needs and suggestions of appropriate interventions to support and stretch learners. The teacher's resource also contains support for preparing and carrying out all the investigations in the practical workbook, including a set of sample results for when practicals aren't possible.

The teacher's resource also contains scaffolded worksheets and unit tests for each chapter. Answers for all components are accessible to teachers for free on the Cambridge GO platform.

The skills-focused workbook has been carefully constructed to help learners develop the skills that they need as they progress through their Cambridge IGCSE Physics course, providing further practice of all the topics in the coursebook. A three-tier, scaffolded approach to skills development enables learners to gradually progress through 'focus', 'practice' and 'challenge' exercises, ensuring that every learner is supported. The workbook enables independent learning and is ideal for use in class or as homework.

The Cambridge IGCSE practical workbook provides learners with additional opportunities for hands-on practical work, giving them full guidance and support that will help them to develop their investigative skills. These skills include planning investigations, selecting and handling apparatus, creating hypotheses, recording and displaying results, and analysing and evaluating data.

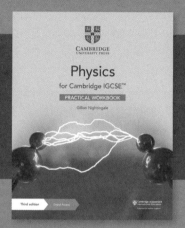

Mathematics is an integral part of scientific study, and one that learners often find a barrier to progression in science. The Maths Skills for Cambridge IGCSE Physics write-in workbook has been written in collaboration with the Association for Science Education, with each chapter focusing on several maths skills that learners need to succeed in their Physics course.

Our research shows that English language skills are the single biggest barrier to learners accessing international science. This write-in workbook contains exercises set within the context of IGCSE Physics topics to consolidate understanding and embed practice in aspects of language central to the subject. Activities range from practising using comparative adjectives in the context of measuring density, to writing a set of instructions using the imperative for an experiment investigating frequency and pitch.

> How to use this book

Throughout this book, you will notice lots of different features that will help your learning. These are explained below. Answers are accessible to teachers for free on the 'supporting resources' area of the Cambridge GO website.

KEY WORDS

Definitions for useful vocabulary are given at the start of each section. You will also find definitions for these words in the Glossary at the back of this book.

Supplement content: In the keyword boxes, Supplement content is indicated with a large arrow, as in this example.

LEARNING INTENTIONS

These set the scene for each exercise, beginning with 'In this exercise you will', and indicate the important concepts.

> In the learning intentions table, Supplement content is indicated with a large arrow and a darker background, as in the example.

KEY EQUATIONS

Important equations which you will need to learn and remember are given in these boxes.

TIPS

The information in these boxes will help you complete the exercises, and give you support in areas that you might find difficult.

Exercises

These help you to practise skills that are important for studying IGCSE Physics.

Questions within exercises fall into one of three types:

- **Focus** questions will help build your basic skills.

- **Practice** questions provide more opportunities for practice, pushing your skills further.

- **Challenge** questions will stretch and challenge you even further.

SELF/PEER ASSESSMENT

At the end of some exercises, you will find opportunities to help you assess your own work, or that of your classmates, and consider how you can improve the way you learn.

Supplement content

Where content is intended for learners who are studying the Supplement content of the syllabus as well as the Core, this is indicated in the main text using the arrow and the bar, as on the left here.

> Introduction

This book has been written to help you increase your understanding of the topics covered in your IGCSE Physics course. The exercises will give you opportunities for the following:

- practice in writing about the ideas that you are studying

- practice in solving numerical and other problems

- practice in thinking critically about experimental techniques and data

- practice in drawing and interpreting diagrams, including graphs.

Most of the exercises are somewhat different from examination questions. This is because they are designed to help you *develop* your knowledge, skills and understanding. Exercises progress through 'focus', 'practice' and 'challenge' stages. The 'focus' questions help to build your foundation skills before gradually giving you more opportunities for practice. The 'challenge' questions aim to stretch you even further.

Spaces have been left for you to write your answers. Some of the diagrams are incomplete, and your task will be to complete them.

Safety

A few practical exercises have been included. These could be carried out at home using simple materials that you are likely to have available to you.

While carrying out such experiments, it is your responsibility to think about your own safety, and the safety of others. If you work sensibly and assess any risks before starting, you should come to no harm. If you are in doubt, discuss what you are going to do with your teacher before you start.

Chapter 1

Making measurements

> Measurements and units

Exercise 1.1

IN THIS EXERCISE YOU WILL:

recall and use the SI units used in physics.

Focus

1 a State the SI units (name and symbol) of the following quantities:

length

....

volume

....

b State the name in words and the symbol for the following:

one thousand metres

....

one-thousandth of a metre

....

c How many?

State the number of centimetres there are in a metre.   ....

State the number of litres there are in a cubic metre.   ....

Practice

2 a State how many cm^2 there are in $1\,m^2$.

....

b State how many m^2 there are in $1\,km^2$.

....

Challenge

3 A cube has sides 3.50 m long. Calculate:

a the surface area of the cube in cm².

....

....

....

....

....

b the volume of the cube in mm³.

....

....

....

....

....

〉 Practical applications

KEY WORD

density: the ratio of mass to volume for a substance

KEY EQUATION

$$\text{density} = \frac{\text{mass}}{\text{volume}}$$

$$\rho = \frac{m}{V}$$

Exercise 1.2

IN THIS EXERCISE YOU WILL:

- practise converting between units
- practise applying the density formula
- apply your understanding of how density affects the behaviour of materials.

Focus

1   **a**   Some data about the density of various solids and liquids are shown in Table 1.1. Complete the fourth column in Table 1.1 by converting each density in kg/m^3 to the equivalent value in g/cm^3. The first two have been done for you.

Material	State / type	Density / kg/m³	Density / g/cm³
water	liquid / non-metal	1000	1.000
ethanol	liquid / non-metal	800	0.800
olive oil	liquid / non-metal	920	
mercury	liquid / metal	13 500	
ice	solid / non-metal	920	
diamond	solid / non-metal	3 500	
cork	solid / non-metal	250	
chalk	solid / non-metal	2 700	
iron	solid / metal	7 900	
tungsten	solid / metal	19 300	
aluminium	solid / metal	2 700	
gold	solid / metal	19 300	

Table 1.1 Densities of various solids and liquids

Two units are used for the densities, kg/m^3 and g/cm^3.

   b   Use the data to explain why ice floats on water.

....

....

2   A cook mixes equal volumes of water and olive oil in a jar. Predict whether one liquid will float on another liquid based on the data given in Table 1.1. Assume that the liquids do not mix.

....

....

Practice

3 A learner wrote: 'These data show that metals are denser than non-metals.' Do you agree? Explain your answer, using the data in Table 1.1.

....

....

....

....

....

4 Using the data in Table 1.1, calculate the mass of a block of gold that measures 20 cm × 15 cm × 10 cm. State your answer in kg.

....

....

....

....

....

5 A metalworker finds a block of silvery metal, weighs it and measures its volume. Here are their results:

      mass of block = 0.270 kg

      volume of block = 14.0 cm³

Calculate the density of the block.

Suggest what metal this might be. ....

Challenge

6   Describe how you could find the density of the metal object in Figure 1.1.

Include:

- the equipment you would use
- how you would use the equipment
- what you would do with the data you collect.

Figure 1.1

....

....

....

....

....

....

....

....

....

Exercise 1.3

IN THIS EXERCISE YOU WILL:

find out how good your pulse would be as a means of measuring time intervals.

Galileo used the regular pulse of his heart as a means of measuring intervals of time, until he noticed that a swinging pendulum was more reliable.

In this exercise, you need to be able to measure the pulse in your wrist. Place two fingers of one hand gently on the inside of the opposite wrist (see Figure 1.2). Press gently at different points until you find the pulse. Alternatively, press two fingers gently under your jawbone on either side of your neck.

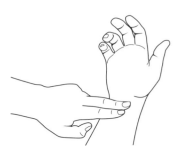

Figure 1.2: Taking a pulse.

You will also need a clock or watch that will allow you to measure intervals of time in seconds.

Focus

1 a Start by timing 10 pulses. (Remember to start counting from zero: 0, 1, 2, 3, ..., 9, 10.) Repeat this several times and record your results in the table.

b Comment on your results.

i How much do your results vary?

....

....

ii Give a possible reason for this: is it difficult to time the pulses or is your heart rate varying?

....

....

c Calculate the average time for one pulse using your results.

....

....

....

Practice

2 Time how long it takes for 50 pulses. Record your results in the table.

3 Calculate the average time for one pulse.

....

....

....

Challenge

4 Investigate how your pulse changes if you take some gentle exercise, for example, by walking briskly, or by walking up and down stairs.

Write up your investigation in the lined space. Use the following as a guide.

- Briefly describe your gentle exercise.

- State the measurements of pulse rate that you have made.

- Comment on whether you agree with Galileo that a pendulum is a better time-measuring instrument than your pulse.

....

....

....

....

....

....

....

....

....

....

....

....

....

....

SELF-ASSESSMENT

Compare your answers to those of your peers. Do you agree with their points?
Are you able to justify yours?

Chapter 2

Describing motion

> Understanding speed

KEY WORDS

speed: the distance travelled by an object in unit time

velocity: speed in a given direction

KEY EQUATIONS

$$speed = \frac{distance}{time}$$

$$v = \frac{s}{t}$$

$$average\ speed = \frac{total\ distance\ travelled}{total\ time\ taken}$$

TIP

There are three mistakes that you can make in calculations:

- rearranging the equation incorrectly

- incorrect or missing unit conversion

- missing or incorrect units.

Practise rearranging equations until you are really happy with it. To test that you are doing it right, pick a calculation where you know all the quantities. For example, in this chapter, we might say 7 m/s would mean 35 metres travelled in 5 seconds. Now rearrange the equation for speed, to make distance, then time, the subject. In each case, having rearranged the equation, substitute the numbers into the equation. If you've done the rearrangement correctly, both sides of the equation should still be equal!

Exercise 2.1

IN THIS EXERCISE YOU WILL:

recall how to measure and calculate the speed of a moving object.

Focus

1 One way to find the speed of an object is to measure the time it takes to travel a measured distance. The table shows the three quantities involved.

Complete the table as follows:

- In the second column, give the SI unit for each quantity (name and symbol).

- In the third column, give some other, non-SI, units for these quantities.

- In the fourth column, name suitable measuring instruments for distance and time.

Quantity	SI unit (name and symbol)	Non-SI units	Measuring instrument
distance			
time			
speed			

TIP
Make sure you are very clear on how to calculate the number of: • metres in a km   • seconds in an hour (or a day, year)   • cm^3 in a m^3.   Take care with units. Always make 'what units should I have here?' the last thing you ask yourself when you've completed a calculation.

2 In the laboratory, the speed of a moving trolley can be found using two light gates. A timer measures the time taken for a trolley to travel from one light gate to the other.

a State what other quantity must be measured to determine the trolley's speed.

....

b Write down the equation used to calculate the speed of the trolley.

....

....

c A trolley takes 0.80 s to travel between two light gates, which are separated by 2.24 m. Calculate its average speed.

....

....

Practice

3   The speed of moving vehicles is sometimes measured using detectors buried in the road.
The two detectors are about 1 m apart. As a vehicle passes over the first detector, an electronic timer starts. As it passes over the second detector, the timer stops.

   a   Explain how the vehicle's speed can then be calculated.

   ....

   ....

   ....

   b   On one stretch of road, any vehicle travelling faster than 25 m/s is breaking the speed limit.
The detectors are placed 1.2 m apart. Calculate the speed of a car that takes 0.050 s to travel this distance. Is it breaking the speed limit?

   ....

   ....

   ....

   c   Calculate the shortest time that a car can take to cross the detectors if it is not to break the speed limit.

   ....

   ....

Challenge

4   Describe briefly how a speed-detection system such as that in Question 3 could be used to light up a warning light whenever a speeding car goes past.

   ....

   ....

   ....

   ....

   ....

PEER ASSESSMENT

Now compare your answers with others. What are the best aspects of their solutions?
How could they improve their solutions?

Exercise 2.2

IN THIS EXERCISE YOU WILL:

- recall and use the equation for speed
- state the difference between speed and velocity.

Focus

1   The table shows the time taken for each of three cars to travel 100 m.
Circle the name of the fastest car. Complete the table by calculating the speed of each car.
Give your answers in m/s and to one decimal place.

Car	Time taken / s	Speed / m/s
red car	4.2	
green car	3.8	
yellow car	4.7	

2   A jet aircraft travels 1200 km in 1 h 20 min.

   a   Calculate how many metres it travels.   ....

   b   Calculate the time for which it travels in minutes/seconds.   ....

   c   Calculate how many seconds it travels.   ....

   d   Calculate its average speed during its flight.

   ....

Practice

3   a   A stone falls 20 m in 2.0 s. Calculate its average speed as it falls.

   ....

   ....

   ....

   b   The stone falls a further 25 m in the next 1.0 s of its fall. Calculate the stone's average
   speed during the 3 s of its fall.

   ....

   ....

   ....

c   Explain why we can only calculate the stone's *average* speed during its fall.

....

....

....

d   State the stone's average velocity during the fall. Explain why you have stated it the way you have.

....

....

Challenge

4   The microwaves used in police speed detection devices travel at 300 000 km/s. Calculate how long it takes for the pulse of microwaves from the device to return to the device after it has been emitted and reflected from an object 200 m away.

....

....

....

> **TIP**
>
> There are many applications of waves being used to calculate distance or speed, where the waves are reflected from an object to calculate how far away it is or how fast it is travelling. Remember that that the distance travelled from source to object and back is TWICE the distance to the object. Another way to look at this is that the time for the waves to travel from the source to the object and back is twice the time to the object.

Exercise 2.3

> **IN THIS EXERCISE YOU WILL:**
>
> practise rearranging the equation for speed.

Focus

1   a   A car is moving at 22 m/s. Calculate how far it will travel in 35 s.

....

....

....

b A swallow (a type of bird) can fly at 25 m/s. Calculate how long it will take to fly 1.0 km.

....

....

....

....

Practice

2 a A high-speed train is 180 m long and is travelling at 50 m/s. Calculate how long it will take to pass a person standing at a level crossing.

....

....

....

....

b Calculate how long the train will take to pass completely through a station whose platforms are 220 m in length.

....

....

....

....

Challenge

3 In a 100 m race, the winner crosses the finishing line in 10.00 s. The runner-up takes 10.20 s.

a Estimate the distance between the winner and the runner-up as the winner crosses the line. Show your method of working.

....

....

....

....

b Explain why your answer can only be an estimate.

....

....

....

⟩ Distance–time graphs

speed = gradient of distance–time graph

Exercise 2.4

IN THIS EXERCISE YOU WILL:

- practise drawing and interpreting distance–time graphs
- perform calculations based on the graphs you have drawn.

Focus

1   Diagrams A–D in Figure 2.1 are distance–time graphs for four moving objects. Complete the table by indicating (in the second column) the graph or graphs that represent the motion described in the first column.

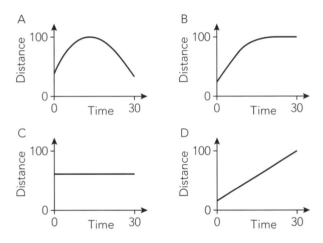

Figure 2.1: Distance–time graphs for four moving objects.

Description of motion	Graph(s)
moving at a steady speed	
stationary (not moving)	
slowing down and stopping	
changing speed	

Practice

2 Table 2.1 shows the distance travelled by a runner during a 100 m race.

Distance / m	0	10.0	25.0	45.0	65.0	85.0	105.0
Time / s	0.0	2.0	4.0	6.0	8.0	10.0	12.0

Table 2.1: Distance travelled by a runner.

a Use the data to draw a distance–time graph on the graph paper provided.

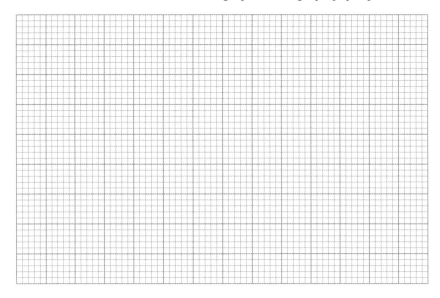

b Use your graph to answer these questions.

  i Determine how far the runner travelled in the first 9.0 s.

  ....

  ii Determine how long the runner took to run the first 50.0 m.

  ....

  iii Determine how long the runner took to complete the 100 m.

  ....

c Use the gradient of your graph to determine the runner's average speed between 4.0 s and 10.0 s. Show the triangle you construct on the graph, in order to find the gradient, where the graph forms the hypoteneuse of that triangle..

  ....

  ....

  ....

  ....

3 On the graph paper provided, sketch a distance–time graph for the car whose journey is described here.

- The car set off at a slow, steady speed for 20 s.

- Then it moved for 40 s at a faster speed.

- Then it stopped at traffic lights for 20 s before setting off again at a slow, steady speed.

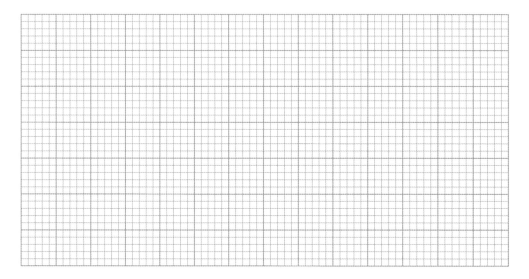

Challenge

4 The graph in Figure 2.2 represents the motion of a bus for part of a journey.

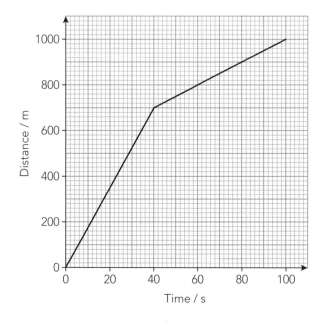

Figure 2.2: Distance–time graph for a bus.

a On the graph, mark the section of the journey where the bus was moving faster.

b   From the graph, calculate:

    i   the speed of the bus when it was moving faster.

       ....

       ....

    ii   the average speed of the bus.

       ....

       ....

> Understanding acceleration

KEY WORD
acceleration: the rate of change of an object's velocity

KEY EQUATION
$$\text{acceleration} = \frac{\text{change in velocity}}{\text{time}}$$ $$a = \frac{\Delta v}{\Delta t}$$

TIP
In an equation the Greek delta Δ represents 'change'. In the equation to determine acceleration, acceleration (a) = change in velocity (Δv) over the time taken, or change in time (Δt).

Exercise 2.5

IN THIS EXERCISE YOU WILL:
• check that you understand acceleration
> recall the equation for acceleration
> practise using the equation for acceleration.

Focus

1   In an advertisement, a car is described like this:

'It can accelerate from 0 km/h to 80 km/h in 10 s.'

Calculate by how much its speed increases in each second (on average). ....

Practice

2   A cyclist is travelling at 4.0 m/s. She speeds up to 16 m/s in a time of 5.6 s.
Calculate her acceleration.

....

....

....

3   A stone falls with an acceleration of 9.8 m/s². Calculate its speed after falling for 3.5 s.

....

....

....

4   On the Moon, gravity is weaker than on Earth. A stone falls with an acceleration of 1.6 m/s² on
the Moon. Calculate how long it will take to reach a speed of 10 m/s.

....

....

....

Challenge

5   A stone is thrown upwards on Earth, where the acceleration of free fall is 9.8 m/s², leaving the
ground at 10 m/s. This is then repeated on Pluto, where gravity is 0.62 m/s². Calculate how much
longer the stone takes to stop on Pluto. Ignore air resistance in your calculations.

....

....

....

〉 Calculating speed and acceleration

KEY WORDS

deceleration: negative acceleration (that is to say, the rate of decrease of velocity)

terminal velocity: the maximum velocity attained by a falling object

---

KEY EQUATIONS

acceleration = gradient of speed–time graph

distance = area under speed–time graph

Exercise 2.6

IN THIS EXERCISE YOU WILL:

- draw and interpret some speed–time graphs

〉 calculate the acceleration of an object from the gradient (slope) of the graph

- calculate the distance travelled from the area under the graph.

Focus

1   Diagrams A–D in Figure 2.3 show speed–time graphs for four moving objects. Complete the table by indicating in the second column the graph or graphs that represent the motion described in the first column.

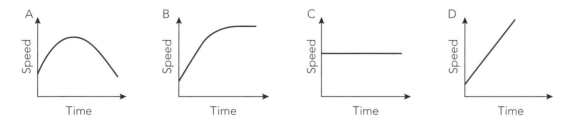

Figure 2.3: Speed–time graphs for four moving objects.

Description of motion	Graph(s)
moving at a steady speed	
speeding up, then slowing down	
moving with constant acceleration	
accelerating to a steady speed	

2   The graph in Figure 2.4 represents the motion of a car that accelerates from rest and then travels at a steady speed.

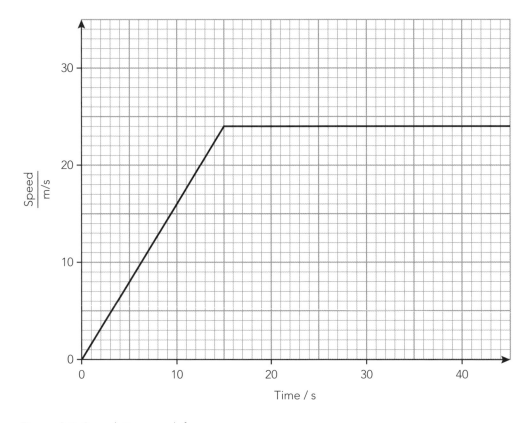

Figure 2.4: Speed–time graph for a car.

Determine the acceleration of the car in the first part of its journey from the graph.

....

Practice

3 **a** On the graph in Question **2**, shade in the area that represents the distance travelled by the car while accelerating. Label this area A.

   b Shade the area that represents the distance travelled by the car at a steady speed. Label this area B.

   c Calculate each of these distances and the total distance travelled by the car.

   [Note: area of a triangle $= \frac{1}{2} \times$ base $\times$ height].

   ....

   ....

   ....

   ....

   ....

Challenge

4 On the graph paper provided, sketch a speed–time graph for the car whose journey is described here.

   • The car set off at a slow, steady speed for 20 s.

   • Then, during a time of 10 s, it accelerated to a faster speed.

   • It travelled at this steady speed for 20 s.

   • Then it rapidly decelerated and came to a halt after 10 s.

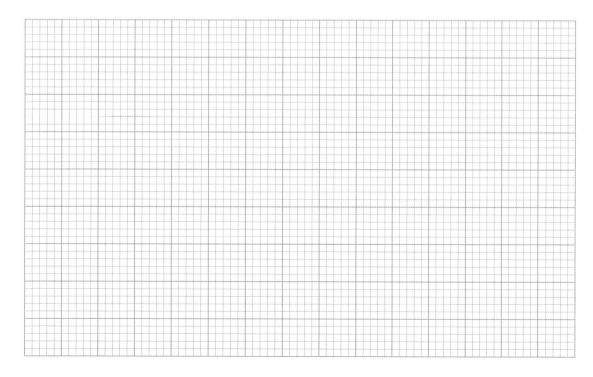

Exercise 2.7

Focus

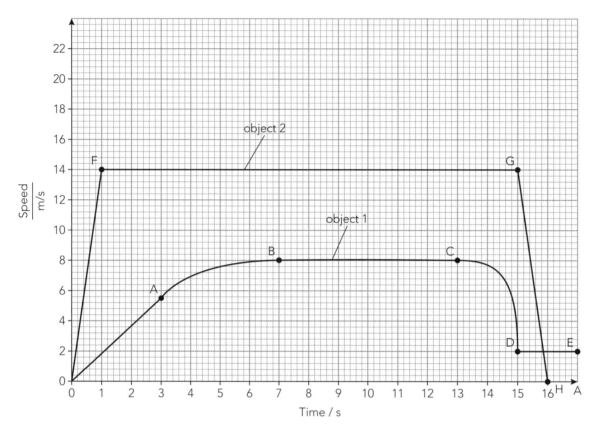

Figure 2.5: The motion of two objects. The motion of object 1 is shown through points A–E, the motion of object 2 is shown through points F–H.

1 Describe the motion of object 1 in Figure 2.5:

a between O and A

....

b between A and B

....

c between B and C

....

d between C and D

....

e between D and E.

....

Practice

2   Calculate the acceleration of object 1 in Figure 2.5:

   a   between O and A

   ....

   b   between A and B

   ....

   c   between B and C

   ....

   d   between C and D

   ....

   e   between D and E

   ....

   f   at exactly 14 seconds.

   ....

Challenge

3   Consider that the two objects in Figure 2.5 are cars in a race.

   a   Explain the shape of section AB.

   ....

   ....

   ....

   ....

   b   Assume that the cars are racing each other. Explain the differences between object 1's
       motion between O and C and object 2's motion between O and G.

   ....

   ....

   ....

   ....

4 Describe and explain the motion of a skydiver when they jump from the aircraft, when they are opening their parachute, and when they are stationary on the ground. You might find it helpful to sketch a speed–time graph before you begin to write your answer.

....

....

....

....

....

....

....

....

....

....

Figure 2.6: A skydiver with an open parachute.

Chapter 3

Forces and motion

> We have lift-off

KEY WORDS
force: the action of one body on a second body that causes its velocity to change
resultant force: the single force that has the same effect on a body as two or more forces

Exercise 3.1

IN THIS EXERCISE YOU WILL:

practise identifying forces, drawing arrows to represent their sizes and their directions.

Focus

1   Fill in the blanks.

A force can change the ……………………… and ……………………… of an object.

Practice

2   Figure 3.1 shows some bodies (objects). Add at least one force arrow to each body, showing a force acting on it. Two force arrows are already shown.

Each force arrow should be labelled to indicate the following:
- the type of force (contact, drag/air resistance, weight/gravitational, push/pull, friction, magnetic)
- the body causing the force
- the body acted on by the force.

For example: the gravitational force of the Earth on the apple (see Figure 3.1).

Figure 3.1: Six situations where forces are acting.

Challenge

3   Why does Figure 3.2 seem to show an impossible situation?

   ....

   ....

   ....

4   Using your knowledge of forces, draw arrows on Figure 3.2 to show where the forces are acting.

Figure 3.2: Why does this seem impossible?

Exercise 3.2

IN THIS EXERCISE YOU WILL:

practise applying your knowledge to predict the effect of forces on objects.

Focus

1   Each diagram in Figure 3.3 shows a body (object) with a single force acting on it. State what effect the force will have in each case.

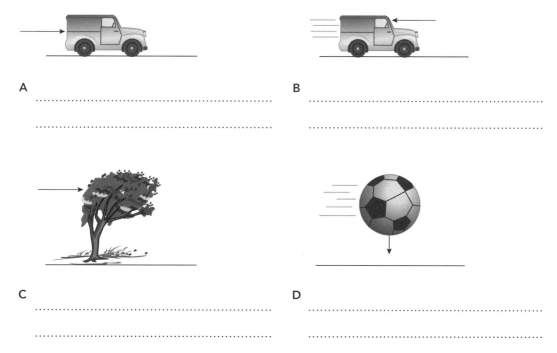

A   ....

   ....

B   ....

   ....

C   ....

   ....

D   ....

   ....

Figure 3.3: Four objects showing a single force acting on each.

Practice

2   A boy slides down a sloping ramp.

  a   Draw a diagram of the boy on the ramp in the space below and add a labelled arrow to show the force of friction that acts on him.

  b   Describe the effect the force will have on the boy's movement.

  ....

  ....

  c   State what other effect friction between two surfaces has.

  ....

Challenge

3   A girl drops her phone from a low height on to the ground and it doesn't break. If she drops it from a first-floor window on to the ground, it does break. Since the weight of the phone has not changed, explain why this is true.

  ....

  ....

Exercise 3.3

IN THIS EXERCISE YOU WILL:

practise working out the resultant force due to several forces acting on an object.

Focus

1   In Table 3.1, the left-hand column shows four objects acted on by different forces. For the same objects in the right-hand column, draw a force arrow to show the resultant force acting on it in each case. Label the arrow with the size of the resultant force.

Forces on object	Resultant force
80N → ☐ ← 45N	☐
60N → ☐ ← 40N 50N ←	☐
20N ↑ 20N → ☐ ← 20N 40N ↓	☐
20N ↑ ↑ 40N 100N → ☐ ← 100N 100N ↓	☐

Table 3.1: A table showing the forces on four bodies.

Practice

2   Describe an effect that a resultant force will have on the motion of an object, for example a car.

    ....

3   Describe the motion of the object if the resultant force falls to zero.

    ....

4   Draw a diagram showing a body (object) with four forces acting on it. Their resultant must be 4 N acting vertically downwards.

Challenge

⟩ **5 a** Calculate the resultant force vector of the 3 N and 2 N forces acting in Figure 3.4.

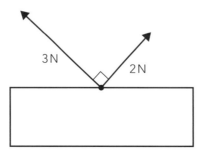

Figure 3.4: Forces acting on an object.

....

....

....

....

b There is a force missing in the diagram. Add an arrow to show the name and direction of the force that must be there, but isn't shown.

⟩ Mass, weight and gravity

KEY EQUATION

gravitational field strength = force per unit mass

$$g = \frac{w}{m}$$

Exercise 3.4

IN THIS EXERCISE YOU WILL:

check your understanding of mass, weight, and gravity's role in weight.

Focus

1 **a** Define weight.

....

b State the equation that connects mass and weight.

....

c State the name of the instrument we use in a laboratory to measure weight.

....

2 State the accepted value of the gravitational field strength on Earth.

....

....

Practice

3 It is often said that astronauts are weightless in the International Space Station, which orbits just outside the atmosphere. State whether you think this is true. Explain your answer.

....

....

....

PEER ASSESSMENT

Now compare your answers to those of your peers. Have they covered all the relevant points? Have you? How could they improve their answers?

Challenge

Figure 3.5: Indoor skydiving.

4   Figure 3.5 shows a man indoor skydiving. Here, he is floating, stationary. Imagine the same man to be floating in deep space. Compare the forces required to move him horizontally in a building on Earth and in deep space. Ignore any difference due to the space suit he would wear in space. Explain your answer.

    ....

    ....

    ....

5   Imagine a creature that lives on Jupiter came to Earth and competed in the Olympic high jump. Consider how they are likely to perform against human competitors and explain your answer. You may want to find out the value of the gravitational field strength on Jupiter.

    ....

    ....

    ....

> Falling

KEY WORDS

uniform gravitational field: a region where the acceleration due to gravity is constant

air resistance: the force on a moving object because it is colliding with air molecules as it moves

TIP

It is a common misconception that when a parachute is opened, the skydiver begins to move upwards. This is because we often see video of this taken by another sky diver. So when the parachute of skydiver 1 opens, that skydiver slows down, but skydiver 2, filming the event, does not. The relative motion of the two looks like skydiver 1 has moved up, when in fact it is just that skydiver 2 hasn't slowed down! They are both falling in the same uniform gravitational field.

Exercise 3.5

IN THIS EXERCISE YOU WILL:

> describe the competing effects of gravity and drag (for example, air resistance).

Galileo is said to have dropped two objects of different masses from the top of the Leaning Tower of Pisa. Figure 3.6 shows the position of the smaller object at equal intervals of time as it fell. You will use this diagram in the following questions.

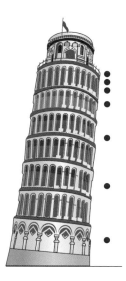

Figure 3.6: Galileo's stone experiment.

Focus

1 The spacing between the dots on Figure 3.6 gradually increases. State what this tells you about the speed of the falling object.

....

....

....

....

Practice

2 a Add dots onto the diagram below to show the pattern you would expect to find for the object with greater mass, but the same surface area (at the same intervals of time).

b What can you say about the accelerations of the two objects?

....

....

....

....

Challenge

3 Galileo's young assistant would probably have enjoyed attaching a parachute to a stone and dropping it from the tower. After a short time, the stone would fall at a steady speed. Add some small crosses onto the diagram below to show the pattern you would expect to see for this.

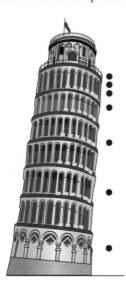

4 The graph in Figure 3.7 shows how the stone's speed would change as it fell. Diagrams A and B are two drawings of the stone, and correspond to points A and B on the graph.

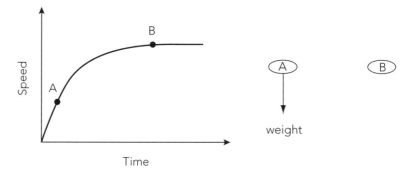

Figure 3.7: A speed–time graph for a falling object.

Diagram A shows the stone's weight.

a   Add a second force arrow to diagram A to show the force of air resistance acting on the stone at point A.

b   Add two force arrows to diagram B to show the forces acting on the stone at this point B in its fall.

c   How would the graph in Figure 3.7 change if the stone was falling through cooking oil, rather than air?

....

....

Force, mass and acceleration

Exercise 3.6

IN THIS EXERCISE YOU WILL:

> practise using the relationship that connects resultant force, mass and acceleration.

Focus

1   a   Complete the table to show the names of these quantities and their SI units.

Quantity	Symbol	SI unit
	F	
	m	
	a	

b   State the equation that connects these three quantities, with F as the subject.

....

c   Rearrange the equation to make m and a the subject.

$m =$ $a =$

Practice

2 Calculate the resultant force needed to give a mass of 20 kg an acceleration of 0.72 m/s².

....

....

....

3 A car of mass 450 kg is acted on by a resultant force of 1575 N. Calculate its acceleration.

....

....

....

4 One way to find the mass of an object is to apply a force to it and measure its acceleration. An astronaut pushes on a spacecraft with a force of 200 N. The spacecraft accelerates at 0.12 m/s². Calculate the mass of the spacecraft.

....

....

....

Challenge

5 a In the space below, draw a falling stone with the following forces acting on it:

- its weight, 8.0 N
- air resistance, 2.4 N.

b Calculate the stone's acceleration. Its mass is 0.80 kg.

....

....

Exercise 3.7

IN THIS EXERCISE YOU WILL:

describe what happens when an object is spun in a circular path.

Focus

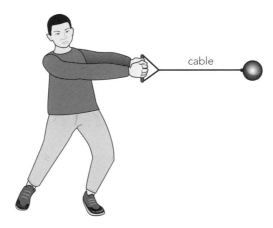

Figure 3.8: An athlete preparing to throw the hammer.

1   **a**   The hammer thrower in Figure 3.8 spins around before releasing the hammer. State what happens to the force he is applying to the hammer as it gets faster. Assume that the radius of the circle and the mass of the hammer remain unchanged.

....

....

....

b   Describe the relative directions of the motion and the force causing the circular motion.

....

....

....

Practice

2   Describe how the force the hammer thrower would need to supply would change if the cable was to be made shorter. Assume the speed of the hammer remains the same before and after the change to the length of the cable.

....

....

....

Challenge

3   Describe how the force changes when any of the following occur.

   a   Increase the mass of the object moving on a circle.

   ....

   b   Increase the radius of the circle the object performs.

   ....

   c   Increase the speed at which the object moves around the circle.

   ....

> The idea of momentum

KEY WORDS

momentum: the product of an object's mass and its velocity

impulse of a force: the product of a force and the time for which it acts

resultant force: the change in momentum per unit time

principle of conservation of momentum: the total momentum of interacting objects is constant provided no net external force acts

KEY EQUATIONS

momentum $p = mv$

impulse − force × time for which the force acts = $F\Delta t$

$$= \Delta(mv)$$

resultant force = change in momentum per unit time

$$F = \frac{\Delta p}{\Delta t}$$

Exercise 3.8

IN THIS EXERCISE YOU WILL:

> calculate the momentum of an object

> calculate the impulse of a force.

TIP

Impulse is a very useful concept. It is common experience that the bigger the resultant force, or the longer it is applied for, the bigger the change in the velocity of an object. Impulse brings those two ideas together into one equation.

Unlike energy, mass and charge, which are always conserved, momentum is only conserved when there are no external forces acting. Most of the time, that isn't actually the case – it is hard to get away from gravity and friction! However, we usually ignore friction, so that momentum is conserved in our questions and we usually have things moving horizontally, so that the forces due to gravity don't have to be considered.

Focus

1   Calculate the momentum of each of the following. Give your answers in kg m/s.

   a   A parachutist of mass 80 kg falling at 15 m/s.

   ....

   ....

   b   A car of mass 500 kg moving at 30 m/s.

   ....

   ....

   c   An insect of mass 5 g flying at 6.0 m/s.

   ....

   ....

2   The parachutist in Question **1a** opens their parachute and their velocity decreases to 5 m/s. Calculate the impulse due to opening the parachute.

   ....

   ....

3   State the relationship between resultant force and momentum.

   ....

Practice

TIP

Remember that momentum is a vector, so the directions of the velocities is important to answer the question correctly.

4 A railway wagon of mass 1000 kg is moving at 9.0 m/s. It collides with a stationary wagon of mass 2000 kg. They stick together and move off along the track.

Answer these questions, using the principle of conservation of momentum, to find out how fast the trolleys move after the collision.

a Calculate the momentum of the moving wagon.

....

....

b Explain why the momentum of the other wagon is zero before it is hit by the moving wagon.

....

....

....

c Calculate the combined mass when the wagons have joined together.

....

d Calculate the combined momentum.

....

e Calculate their combined speed.

....

....

....

f Calculate the impulse of the wagon that was initially stationary.

....

....

g The impact took 0.1 seconds. Calculate the acceleration of the 2000 kg wagon.

....

....

....

h How would this value of acceleration change if the coupling mechanism was spring-loaded, so that the collision took place over a longer period of time?

....

....

....

....

....

....

....

....

....

....

....

....

Challenge

5   A car of mass 500 kg is moving at 10 m/s. When the driver decides to accelerate, a force of 200 N acts on the car for 12 s.

Answer these questions to find out how fast the car moves after it has accelerated.

a   Calculate the impulse that makes the car accelerate.

....

....

....

b   Calculate the momentum of the car before it accelerates.

....

....

....

c   Calculate the momentum of the car after it has accelerated.

....

....

....

d   Calculate the speed of the car after it has accelerated.

....

....

....

e The car now collides with a wall and stops in a time of 5 ms. Calculate the average resultant force on the car to achieve this.

....

....

....

> Scalars and vectors

Exercise 3.9

IN THIS EXERCISE YOU WILL:

> practise adding vectors by scale drawing and by calculation
> check that you remember which quantities are vectors and which are scalars.

TIP

The two things to remember about drawing scale diagrams are:

1 measure VERY carefully

2 draw VERY accurately.

If you don't do these two things, even if you do everything else right, your answer may be outside the acceptable range.

Focus

1 Complete the table, showing which quantities are vectors and which are scalars.

Quantity	Vector or scalar
force	
distance	
temperature	

Quantity	Vector or scalar
mass	
gravitational field strength	
velocity	
weight	
energy	
speed	
electric field strength	
time	
temperature	

2   Here is a vector diagram of two forces acting on an object:

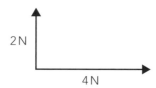

Figure 3.9: Vector diagram showing forces of 2 N and 4 N acting on an object.

a   Redraw Figure 3.9 to show how to find the resultant vector.

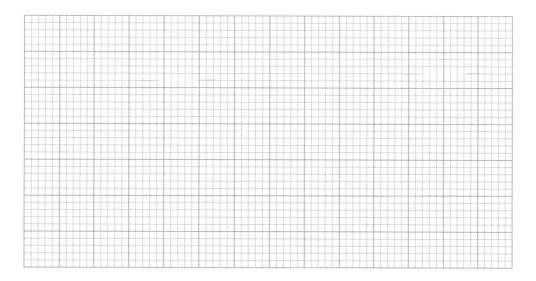

b   As well as its size, state what else you must quote when talking about a vector.

   ....

3   Find the resultant vector in Figure 3.10:

a   by scale drawing

b   by calculation.

Figure 3.10: Free body force diagram showing forces of 7 N and 10 N acting on an object.

a

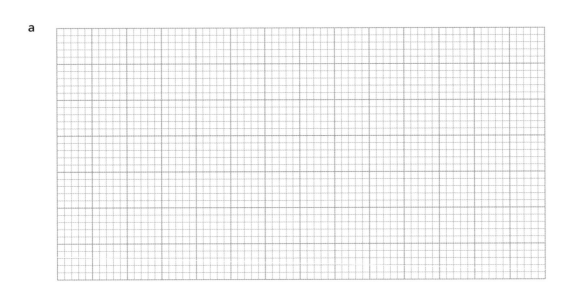

b   ....

   ....

Practice

4 Find the resultant vector in Figure 3.11:

   a by scale drawing

   b by calculation.

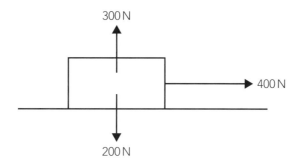

Figure 3.11: Free body force diagram showing three forces of 200 N, 300 N and 400 N acting on an object.

a

b ....

....

Challenge

5 Find the resultant force vector in Figure 3.12:

a by scale drawing

b by calculation.

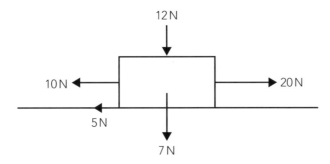

Figure 3.12: Free body force diagram showing five forces acting on an object.

a

b ....
....

Chapter 4

Turning effects

> The moment of a force

> **KEY WORDS**
>
> **equilibrium:** when no net force and no net moment act on a body
>
> **moment of a force:** the turning effect of a force about a point

Exercise 4.1

> **IN THIS EXERCISE YOU WILL:**
>
> check your understanding of simple turning effects and of equilibrium.

Focus

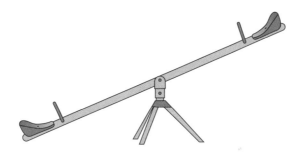

Figure 4.1: A playground see-saw.

1   Explain how a playground see-saw, like the one in Figure 4.1, can balance.

    ....

    ....

2   A body (object) is in equilibrium.

    a   State the resultant force on the body.

        ....

    b   State the resultant turning effect on the body.

        ....

Practice

3 **a** Figure 4.2 shows a wheelbarrow with a heavy load of soil. Add an arrow to show how you could lift the left-hand end of the barrow with the smallest force possible. Remember to indicate clearly the direction of the force.

Figure 4.2: A wheelbarrow.

b How do you know that the wheelbarrow is in equilibrium?

....

Challenge

4 **a** Figure 4.3 shows a beam balanced on a pivot. Add arrows to show the following forces:

- A 100 N force pressing downwards on the beam that will have the greatest possible clockwise turning effect. Label this force A.

- A 200 N force pressing downwards on the beam that will have an anticlockwise turning effect equal in size to the turning effect of force A. Label this force B.

Figure 4.3: A uniform beam, balanced on a pivot at the centre of the beam.

b What other forces are acting, as well as the two in part **a**, to keep the beam in equilibrium?

....

....

c Why can we ignore these in calculating moments about the pivot?

....

› Calculating moments

KEY EQUATION

moment of a force = force × perpendicular distance from pivot to force

TIP

Remember that we add all the clockwise moments together and all the anticlockwise moments together. This is the key thing NOT whether the forces are on the left or the right of the pivot. For example, a force on the left of the pivot will have a clockwise moment, if it acts upwards, but an anticlockwise moment if it acts downwards.

Exercise 4.2

IN THIS EXERCISE YOU WILL:

check your understanding of how to calculate moments.

Focus

1   Fill in the blanks.

The ………………… of a force is the turning effect of the force. It is calculated by multiplying

the size of the force by the ………………… distance of the ……… ……… …………………

from the pivot.

Practice

2   For each of the situations in Figure 4.4, calculate the missing force or distance so that the beams are in equilibrium.

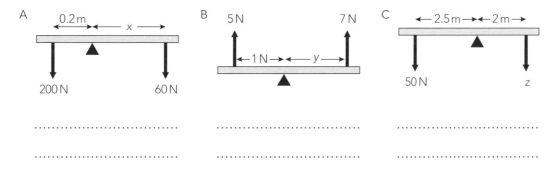

....

....

Figure 4.4: Three situations, showing beams balanced with different combinations of moments.

Challenge

3   In Question **2**, we did not consider the weight of the beam. On the assumption that the beam is uniform and pivoted in the middle, state why you think this is this reasonable.

....

....

Exercise 4.3

IN THIS EXERCISE YOU WILL:

> apply the principle of moments to other situations.

Focus

1   In Figure 4.5, all the forces are of equal size.

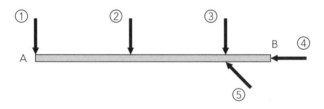

Figure 4.5: Five forces of equal size, acting at different points along a uniform beam.

a   State the force with the greatest moment about point A.

....

b   State the force that has no moment about point B.

....

Practice

2   **a**   Calculate the moment about the pivot of each force in Figure 4.6. Write your answers in the table.

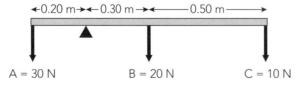

Figure 4.6: A uniform beam pivoted off-centre.

Force	Moment / Nm	Clockwise or anticlockwise?
A		
B		
C		

b   State which force must be removed if the beam is to be balanced.

....

3   In Figure 4.7, the beam is balanced (in equilibrium). Calculate the size of force *F*.

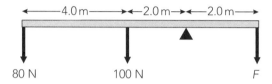

Figure 4.7: A uniform beam pivoted off-centre, with an unknown force.

....

....

Challenge

4   Look at Figure 4.8.

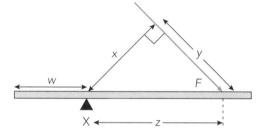

Figure 4.8: A force acting at an acute angle to a uniform beam.

a   State which distance should be used in calculating the moment of force *F* about point X.

....

b   Explain why you chose this distance for your answer.

....

....

....

> Stability and centre of gravity

KEY WORDS

centre of gravity: the point at which the mass of an object can be considered to be concentrated

Exercise 4.4

IN THIS EXERCISE YOU WILL:

check your understanding of stability and the factors that affect it.

Focus

1   State and explain the condition that means an object will topple (fall over).

   ....

   ....

   ....

   ....

Practice

2   Figure 4.9 shows an object that is fairly stable. Its centre of gravity is marked with a dot.

Figure 4.9: A stone on a flat surface.

   a   On the left of this object, draw an object that is more stable. Mark its centre of gravity.

   b   On the right of this object, draw an object that is less stable. Mark its centre of gravity.

3 Figure 4.10 shows two objects that are not very stable. The centre of gravity of each is marked with a dot.

State the two vertical forces that act on each of these objects.

Upward force ....

Downward force ....

4 a Draw arrows on each object in Figure 4.10 showing the two forces acting on it.

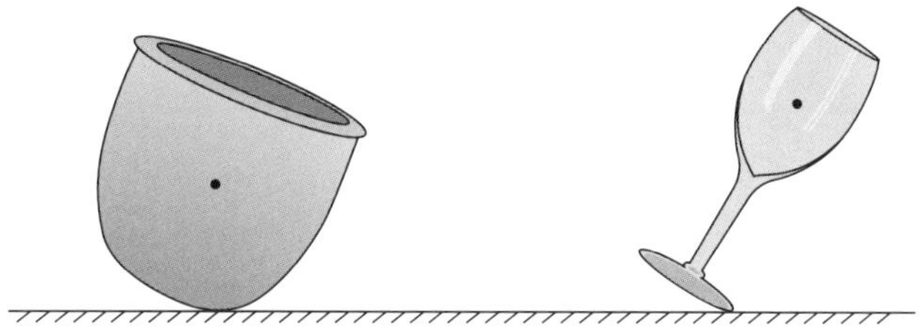

Figure 4.10: A plant pot and a water glass, both tilted to one side.

b Decide whether each object will fall over. Explain your answer.

....

....

....

....

....

....

....

....

....

....

Challenge

TIP
Whether or not an object topples (falls over) is all about whether the moment of the weight tends to pull the object further over, or tends to cause it to fall back where it was. So, as the object starts to fall over, if the line along which weight acts falls outside the base (the wheels of the car in these examples), it will topple. If it falls inside the wheels, then it tends to pull the car back on to four wheels.

5 Explain, using your knowledge of stability, which of the two cars in Figure 4.11 you would expect to be able to go around a corner at the highest speed, whilst keeping all its wheels on the road.

Car A   **Car B**

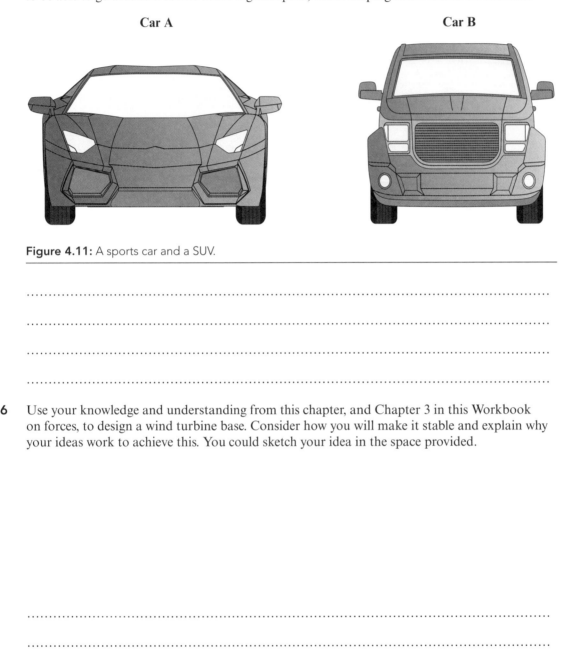

Figure 4.11: A sports car and a SUV.

....

....

....

....

6 Use your knowledge and understanding from this chapter, and Chapter 3 in this Workbook on forces, to design a wind turbine base. Consider how you will make it stable and explain why your ideas work to achieve this. You could sketch your idea in the space provided.

....

....

....

....

PEER ASSESSMENT

Now compare your answer to those of others. Is there anything they could add to improve it? Is there anything you could have added?

> Chapter 5
Forces and matter

> Stretching springs

KEY EQUATION

$F = kx$, where F = applied force (in N), k = spring constant (in N/m), x = extension (in m)

so $k = \dfrac{F}{x}$

Exercise 5.1

IN THIS EXERCISE YOU WILL:

- describe an experiment to investigate the relationship between the load on a spring and the extension of that spring
- practise plotting a graph and drawing conclusions from it.

Focus

1. Describe how you would carry out an experiment to investigate the relationship between the load on a spring and the extension of that spring. Draw a diagram of your experimental arrangement in the space provided on the next page.

....

....

....

....

....

Practice

2 **a** A learner carried out an experiment to stretch a spring. Table 5.1 shows her results.

Complete the third column of the table.

TIP
Remember that the extension is the TOTAL increase in length from the unstretched value.

Load / N	Length / cm	Extension / mm
0	25.0	
1.0	25.4	
2.0	25.8	
3.0	26.2	
4.0	26.6	
5.0	27.0	
6.0	27.4	
7.0	27.8	
8.0	28.5	
9.0	29.2	
10.0	29.9	

Table 5.1: Results of spring experiment.

b From the data in Table 5.1, estimate the force needed to produce an extension of 1.0 cm.

....

c   On the graph paper grid, draw an extension–load graph for the spring.

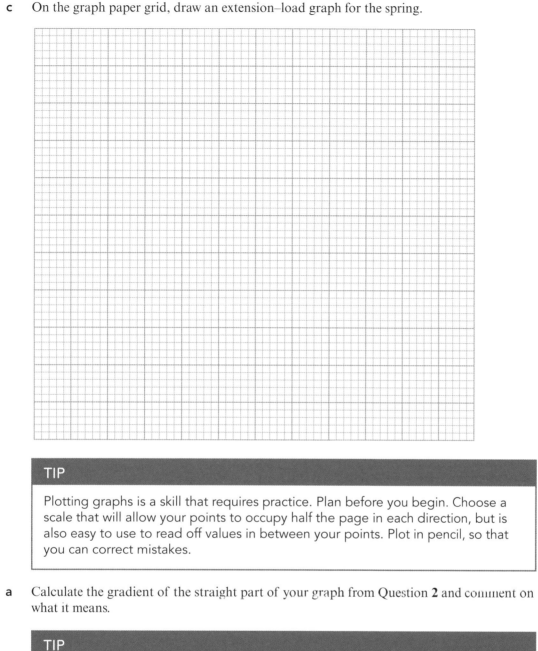

> **TIP**
>
> Plotting graphs is a skill that requires practice. Plan before you begin. Choose a scale that will allow your points to occupy half the page in each direction, but is also easy to use to read off values in between your points. Plot in pencil, so that you can correct mistakes.

3   a   Calculate the gradient of the straight part of your graph from Question **2** and comment on what it means.

> **TIP**
>
> When you've calculated a gradient, always think 'What should the units of this value be?' This will help to ensure you assign units when you should and also help you to understand what the gradient actually means.

....

....

....

b From your graph, estimate the load at the limit of proportionality.

....

Challenge

4 Steel cables can behave like springs when stretched. One of the biggest challenges for making very tall buildings (over 100 storeys) is the limitations in cable technology for the elevators. Using your knowledge of extensions and springs, research what these limitations are and pick one to explore in depth. Then research what the solution could be.

Is there a solution? Write a one page report on this to share with your class.

> **TIP**
>
> One place you might like to think about is Mponeng gold mine in South Africa. This is one of the world's deepest mines (at the time of writing). If you wish to choose this as your example, you could describe the challenges for getting miners in and out of the mine.

> **PEER ASSESSMENT**
>
> Now compare your report with those of your peers. Does their report answer the question? Are there things they could do to improve it? What are the best aspects of the report?

Exercise 5.2

Focus

1 Add mathematical symbols in the wide spaces to turn the following words into an equation. There are **two** different ways to do it. Find both.

| stretched length | original length | extension |

| stretched length | original length | extension |

Practice

2 A spring has a spring constant of 12 N/m and extends 10 cm under load. Calculate the applied load.

....

....

....

....

3   A force of 10 N causes a spring to extend by 3 cm. Calculate the spring constant.

   ....

   ....

   ....

   ....

4   Four people, each of mass 90 kg, get into a car with four wheels, and it is seen that the car body moves 1.1 cm down towards the ground. Calculate the spring constant of the suspension springs that support the car on its wheels.

   ....

   ....

   ....

   ....

Challenge

5   If two of the springs from Question **2** were used, describe how the spring constant would compare if they were connected:

Figure 5.1: Two springs (**a**) in series, (**b**) in parallel.

a   in series, as in Figure 5.1a.

b   in parallel, as in Figure 5.1b. Explain your answer in each case.

   ....

   ....

   ....

   ....

   ....

   ....

   ....

> Pressure

KEY WORD

pressure: the force acting per unit area at right angles to a surface

KEY EQUATIONS

$$pressure = \frac{force}{area}$$

$$p = \frac{F}{A}$$

pressure in a liquid, $\Delta p = \rho g \Delta h$

Exercise 5.3

IN THIS EXERCISE YOU WILL:

- practise carrying out pressure calculations
- apply your knowledge of the pressure equation to real situations.

Focus

1   The equation $p = \dfrac{F}{A}$ is used to calculate pressure.

   a   Complete the table to show the name of each quantity and the SI unit (name and symbol) of each quantity.

Quantity	Symbol	SI unit
	F	
	p	
	A	

   b   Rearrange the equation to make F and A the subject.

   $F =$ $A =$

2 It is dangerous to stand on the icy surface of a frozen pond or lake.

a Explain why it is more dangerous to stand on one foot than on both feet.

....

....

....

....

b Describe how a wild animal could move across the ice in such a way as to minimise the danger of falling through.

....

....

....

Practice

3 Calculate the pressure when a force of 200 N presses on an area of 0.40 m^2.

....

....

....

4 The pressure inside a car tyre is 250 kPa (250 000 Pa). Calculate the total force exerted on the inner surface of the tyre if its surface area is 0.64 m^2.

....

....

....

Challenge

Figure 5.2: A rocket being transported to the launch pad.

5   The rocket in Figure 5.2 is 111 m high and has a mass of 3 100 000 kg. Explain how the vehicle transporting it is adapted to carry such a load.

....

....

....

....

Exercise 5.4

IN THIS EXERCISE YOU WILL:

> practise using the pressure in liquids equation.

Focus

1   State the equation linking pressure in a liquid to the depth of the liquid.

....

Practice

2   Calculate the pressure at the bottom of an oil storage tank of depth 2.50 m. The oil has a density of 980 kg/m^3, and $g = 10$ m/s^2.

....

....

....

3 **a** Estimate the height of the Earth's atmosphere using the following data:

atmospheric pressure = 100 kPa; density of air = 1.29 kg/m^3.

....

....

....

b Explain why this can only be an estimate.

....

....

Challenge

4 Objects submerged in a liquid appear to have a smaller weight. One way to explain this is that there is a difference in pressure on the top and bottom surfaces. Knowing the relationship between pressure and force, from the key equations box, use Figure 5.3 to calculate the difference in the weight of the block in water compared to its weight in air.

The block is a cuboid, with horizontal faces of area = 2 m^2.

The depth of the block = 1 m.

It is submerged in water, of density = 1000 kg/m^3.

The bottom of the block is at a depth of 6 m.

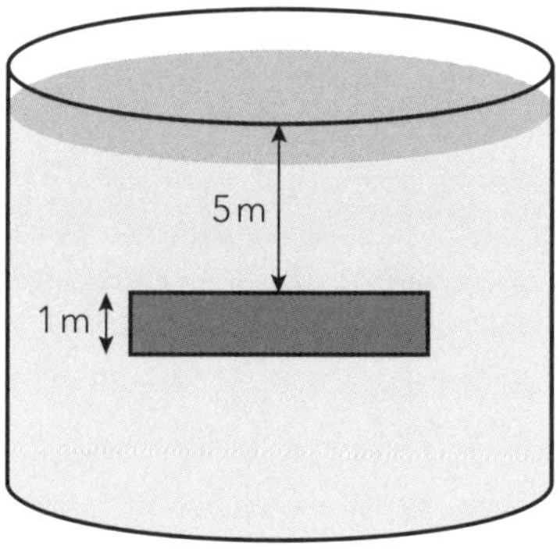

Figure 5.3: A block submerged in water.

....

....

....

....

....

....

Chapter 6

Energy stores and transfers

> Energy stores

KEY WORDS

principle of conservation of energy: the total energy of interacting objects is constant provided no net external force acts

chemical potential energy: energy stored in chemical substances and which can be released in a chemical reaction

gravitational potential energy: the energy stored in an object that is raised up against the force of gravity

nuclear potential energy: energy stored in the nucleus of an atom

Sankey diagram: a diagram to show all the energy transfers taking place in a process using arrows. Each transfer is shown by a separate arrow. The width of the arrows represents the amount of energy being transferred

---

Exercise 6.1

IN THIS EXERCISE YOU WILL:

- check that you know what energy stores and transfers are
- practise identifying energy stores and transfers in everyday situations
- apply the principle of conservation of energy to energy flow diagrams.

Focus

1   Sometimes, energy is being stored (chemical energy is an example). Sometimes, energy is being transferred from one object to another or from place to place.

Complete the table. The first example has been done for you.

Description	Store of energy
energy in a stretched spring/elastic	*elastic potential*
energy in the nucleus of a uranium atom	
energy in diesel fuel	
energy of a ball held above your head	
energy of a hot cup of coffee	

2   Figure 6.1 shows a rocket being launched into space, and the energy transfers that are involved.

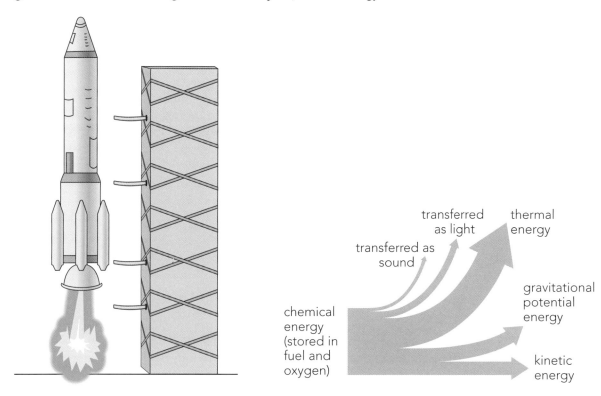

Figure 6.1: A rocket being launched.

In the table, explain how you know that each of these energy changes is happening. The first one has been done for you.

Energy transfer: chemical energy to …	How we can tell
sound	*The rocket launch is very noisy.*
light	
thermal energy	
gravitational potential energy	
kinetic energy	

Practice

3   Explain how the energy flow diagram in Figure 6.1 shows that the principle of conservation of energy is obeyed in these energy changes.

....

....

....

4   A washing machine has a motor that turns the drum. In a particular washing machine, the motor is supplied with 1500 J of energy each second. Of this, 1200 J of energy is used to turn the drum. The rest is wasted as thermal energy. Draw an energy flow diagram for the washing machine.

5   An energy flow diagram can be used to represent energy changes. Figure 6.2 shows the energy changes in a light bulb each second. A coal-fired power station is used to provide the electricity.

Figure 6.2: Energy flow diagram for a light bulb.

On the diagram, in the correct place, write in the amount of light produced each second.

Challenge

6   A learner argues that a car running on petrol or diesel is more efficient in winter than in summer. Explain why the learner might say this.

....

....

....

7   a   Draw a Sankey Diagram to show the following. A low-energy light bulb is 85% efficient and the wasted energy is thermal. It receives power from a National Grid that is 92% efficient. It is supplied by a power station that is 60% efficient. Assume all wasted energy is thermal. Show your diagram with an input energy of 100J.

b   Calculate the overall efficiency of the system from generation to light bulb.

....

....

> Energy transfers and efficiency

KEY WORD

efficiency: the fraction of energy that is transferred to a useful form

KEY EQUATIONS

$$\text{efficiency of a device} = \frac{\text{useful energy output}}{\text{total energy input}} \times 100\%$$

$$\text{efficiency of a device} = \frac{\text{useful power output}}{\text{total power input}} \times 100\%$$

Exercise 6.2

IN THIS EXERCISE YOU WILL:

> check that you understand the concept of efficiency.

TIP

Efficiency is the proportion (NOT the amount) of total input that is transferred usefully.

You'll see this expressed in terms of energy, work and power, but work and energy are the same thing, and power is the rate of doing work. You can ask yourself 'What is the purpose of this device?' in order to decide what's useful. For example, a light bulb exists to produce light, so the thermal energy it produces is not generally considered useful.

Focus

1 A washing machine has a motor that turns the drum. In a particular washing machine, the motor is supplied with 1200 J of energy each second. Of this, 900 J of energy is used to turn the drum. The rest is wasted as thermal energy.

Calculate the amount of energy wasted each second.

....

....

2 **a** Calculate the efficiency of the motor in the washing machine. Give your answer as a percentage.

....

....

b Explain why we say that energy from the washing machine is 'wasted' as thermal energy.

....

....

Practice

3 • A gas-fired power station is supplied with 1000 MJ of energy each second and produces 450 MJ of electrical energy.

• A coal-fired power station is supplied with 600 MJ of energy each second and produces 150 MJ of electrical energy.

a Which power station is more efficient? ....

b Calculate the efficiency of each power station.

....

....

4 Figure 6.3 shows the energy transfers in a light bulb each second. A coal-fired power station is used to provide the electricity.

Figure 6.3: Energy flow diagram for a light bulb.

Calculate the efficiency of the bulb.

....

....

Challenge

5 **a** Draw an energy flow diagram for the following power transmission system:
- solar panel (20% efficient)
- solar inverter (converts DC to AC, 95% efficient)
- step-up transformer (95% efficient)
- overhead power transmission cable (95% efficient)
- step-down transformer (95% efficient).

Assume that there is 1000 J of solar energy arriving at the solar panel.

b What is the overall efficiency of the power transmission system?

....

....

> Energy conservation and energy calculations

KEY WORDS

kinetic energy (k.e.): the energy stored in a moving object

KEY EQUATIONS

kinetic energy $= \dfrac{1}{2} \times$ mass $\times$ speed^2

$E_k = \dfrac{1}{2}mv^2$

change in gravitational potential energy = weight $\times$ change in height

$\Delta E_p = mg\Delta h$

Exercise 6.3

IN THIS EXERCISE YOU WILL:

> recall and use the equations to calculate kinetic energy and change in gravitational potential energy

> apply these equations with the principle of conservation of energy to more complex problems (see Question 5).

TIP

Remember that, when you are calculating the change in k.e., when an object goes from v_1 m/s to v_2 m/s, it is $\frac{1}{2}mv_2^2 - \frac{1}{2}mv_1^2$, NOT $\frac{1}{2}m(v_2 - v_1)^2$.

Focus

1 State the equations for kinetic energy and change in gravitational potential energy, with mass as the subject for each.

   a k.e.: $m =$ ....

   b change in g.p.e.: $m =$ ....

Practice

2 Calculate the kinetic energy of a car of mass 600 kg travelling at 25 m/s.

   ....

3 A walker carrying a 20 kg backpack climbs to the top of a mountain 2500 m high. Calculate the gain in gravitational potential energy of the pack.

   (Acceleration due to gravity $g = 10$ m/s^2).

   ....

Challenge

4 The car in Question **2** slows down to a speed of 12 m/s. By how much has its kinetic energy decreased?

   ....

5 A girl throws a ball upwards (Figure 6.4). The ball has a mass of 0.20 kg and it leaves her hand with a speed of 8.0 m/s. Determine how high it will rise.

Figure 6.4: A girl throwing a ball into the air.

....

....

....

> TIP
>
> **Step 1:** Calculate the k.e. of the ball as it leaves the girl's hand.
>
> **Step 2:** When the ball reaches its highest point, it no longer has any k.e. and its energy has been transferred to g.p.e.
>
> So now we can write:
>
> **g.p.e. at highest point = k.e. at lowest point**
>
> mgh **= k.e.**
>
> Rearranging gives:
>
> $$h = \frac{k.e.}{mg}$$

6   In a game, a toy car, which is initially stationary, slides down a slope. The top of the slope is 2.0 m higher than the foot of the slope. Determine how fast the car will be moving when it reaches the foot. (Assume that all of its g.p.e. is transferred to k.e.).

....

....

....

> Chapter 7
Energy resources

> The energy we use

Exercise 7.1

IN THIS EXERCISE YOU WILL:

- recall which resources are renewable and non-renewable
- discuss the advantages and disadvantages of different types of energy resources.

Focus

1 Complete the table as follows:

- in the second column, write the name of the type of energy resource.
- in the third column, indicate whether the resource is renewable or non-renewable.

The first example has been done for you.

Description	Energy resource	Renewable or non-renewable?
wood	*biofuel*	*renewable*
natural gas		
coal		
splitting of uranium nuclei		
hydrogen nuclei combine to release energy		
sunlight captured to make electricity or heat water		

Description	Energy resource	Renewable or non-renewable?
underground hot rocks used to heat water		
moving air turns a turbine		
water running downhill turns a turbine		

TIP

Renewable is about being able to replace something at least as fast as we use it. It is NOT about being able to re-use it.

TIP

Take care not to confuse the spelling of 'fission' and 'fusion'. Fusion spelled 'fussion' is neither one nor the other!

Practice

2   Draw a diagram (with labels and notes) to explain why hydroelectric power can be described as renewable.

Challenge

3   Compare the energy resources by completing the table. You will need to conduct research to find much of the missing information.

Resource	Renewable?	Cost per MWh of electricity	Scale of production LS = Large Scale, > 1GW; SS = Small Scale	Environmental impact	Reliability
nuclear fission					
solar					
geothermal					
hydroelectric					
wind					
wave					
tidal					

Exercise 7.2

IN THIS EXERCISE YOU WILL:

consider wind power in some detail.

Focus

1   Figure 7.1 shows how much electricity was generated worldwide from the wind from 1996 to 2018. (The units of energy are GWh, or gigawatt-hours. One gigawatt is 10^9 watts.) Table 7.1 shows the top ten countries that contributed most to this total in 2018.

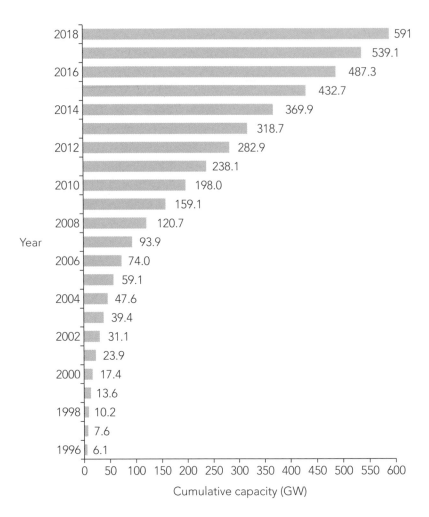

Figure 7.1: Graph of global wind power capacity.

Country	Global wind power 2018 / %	Country	Global wind power 2018 / %
China	44.3	Brazil	3.7
United States	14.7	France	3
Germany	6.1	Mexico	1.8
India	4.2	Sweden	1.4
United Kingdom	4	Canada	1.1

Table 7.1: Global wind power, top ten countries.

Source: *Global Wind Energy Council*

Study Figure 7.1 and Table 7.1, and then read each of the statements below. Decide whether each statement is TRUE or FALSE. If a statement is FALSE, cross out the incorrect word(s) and write the correct word(s) in the space below.

Here is an example to help you:

2005

The amount of electricity generated from the wind reached 50 GWh in ~~2001~~.

~~TRUE~~/FALSE

i   The amount of electricity generated from the wind has increased every year since 1996.

TRUE / FALSE

ii   The amount of electricity generated from the wind exceeded 100 GWh in 2006.

TRUE / FALSE

iii   The amount of electricity generated from the wind doubled between 2002 and 2005.

TRUE / FALSE

iv   The top three countries generate more than 50% of the world's wind energy.

TRUE / FALSE

v   The UK makes less use of wind energy than France.

TRUE / FALSE

Practice

2   Think about the area where you live. Suggest a good place to put a wind turbine to generate as much electricity as possible. Give reasons for your suggestion.

....

....

....

....

Challenge

3   State objections that might be raised to using wind power as a major source of our electricity.

....

....

....

....

....

....

> Energy from the Sun

KEY WORDS

fossil fuel: a material, formed from long-dead material, used as a fuel

nuclear fusion: the process by which energy is released by the joining together of two small light nuclei to form a new heavier nucleus

Exercise 7.3

IN THIS EXERCISE YOU WILL:

> describe the energy we get directly and indirectly from the Sun in some detail

> discuss the difference between nuclear fission and fusion and how we might use nuclear fusion on Earth to generate electricity in the future.

Focus

1   What do we use to transfer the energy from the Sun into electricity?

....

2   In the table, the first column lists some energy resources. In the second column, indicate with a tick (✓) if the energy of the resource comes originally from the Sun. Indicate with a cross (✗) if it doesn't. The first one has been done for you.

Energy resource	Originally from the Sun?
wood	✓
fossil fuels	
nuclear power	
tidal power	
wind power	
hydroelectric power	
wave	
geothermal	
sunlight	

Practice

3 Explain why, when we burn coal, the energy released originally came from the Sun.

....

....

....

....

....

4 Fission and fusion are two processes that release energy when changes happen in the nuclei of atoms. The table lists some features of these processes. Some relate to fission and some to fusion.

Write 'fission' or 'fusion' or 'both' in the second column of the table as appropriate.

Feature	Fission, fusion or both?
large nuclei split into two	
two small nuclei join together	
energy is released	
used in a uranium-fuelled power station	
the energy source of the Sun	
helium can be a product	

Challenge

5 Describe the main issues with using solar energy to generate the Earth's electricity.

....

....

....

....

....

....

....

....

6 Research: Nuclear fusion on Earth.

There are two main approaches to trying to make nuclear fusion happen on Earth.

Inertial confinement fusion (ICF) uses lasers to heat the fuel.

Magnetic confinement fusion (MCF) uses magnetic fields to contain and control the fuel.

ICF is being researched at the National Ignition Facility at the Lawrence Livermore National Laboratory in the USA.

MCF is taking place in Europe, in England and the south of France.

Find out about these two approaches to fusion. For each, write down:

- how they work

- why they need to reach the temperatures they do

- what is holding them back from making fusion a realistic energy source for generating electricity on Earth

- what their prospects are over the next 10 years.

This is a really exciting part of science and engineering that offers young scientists (like you) the chance to make a discovery that will change the world. Someone will make fusion work. Will that be you?

....

....

....

....

....

....

....

....

....

....

....

....

....

....

....

....

....

....

....

....

....

....

....

....

....

....

....

....

....

....

....

....

....

....

....

....

....

....

....

PEER ASSESSMENT

Compare your work to that of others. Do they have any good points that you didn't consider? What could they do to improve their answer?

> Chapter 8
Work and power

> Doing work

KEY WORDS

energy: the capacity to do work

doing work: transferring energy

joule (J): the SI unit of work or energy

work done: the amount of energy transferred

TIP

You will come across work, energy and power in different areas of the course, but they are the same every time you see them. Work and energy are just two words for the same thing. Power is the rate of doing work, which is the rate of energy transfer.

Exercise 8.1

IN THIS EXERCISE YOU WILL:

- check your understanding of work
- practise explaining the energy transfers involved when work is done in some everyday situations.

Focus

1 State the relationship between work and energy.

   ....

Practice

2 Complete these sentences:

   An apple falls from a tree. The force acting on the apple to make it fall is ....

   As it falls, its speed .... This shows that its .... energy store is increasing.

   If this increase is by 2.0 joule (J), the work done on it is ....J.

3 The girl in Figure 8.1 is raising a heavy load.

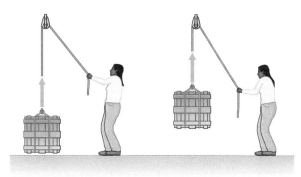

Figure 8.1: A girl lifting a heavy load using a pulley.

a Explain how you can tell that the load's energy is increasing.

....

....

b Explain where this energy comes from.

....

....

c Explain how the energy is transferred to the load.

....

....

4 In Figure 8.2, the 20 N force does more work than the 10 N force. State **two** ways that you can tell this.

Figure 8.2: The forces acting on a block.

....

....

....

....

Challenge

5   Using the concept of work, explain why it is more difficult to walk on an icy surface than on a clean, dry, unfrozen surface.

....

....

....

....

....

> Calculating work done

Exercise 8.2

IN THIS EXERCISE YOU WILL:

practise using the expression for mechanical work done by a force.

Focus

1   The learner in Figure 8.3 is pulling a load up a slope.

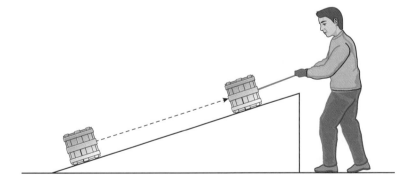

Figure 8.3: A learner pulling a load up a slope.

a   What instrument could be used to measure the force F that pulls the load?

....

b   On Figure 8.3, mark the distance x that must be measured in order to calculate the work done by the force.

c   Write the equation used to calculate the work done by the force.

....

d   The learner changes the angle of the slope four times. In the space below, draw up a suitable table that could be used to record the measurements and to calculate the work done by the force.

Practice

2   A boy pushes a heavy box along the ground. His pushing force is 75 N. He pushes it for a distance of 4.0 m.

Calculate the work done by the boy in pushing the box.

....

....

3   On a building site, a crane lifts a load of bricks. The lifting force is 2500 N and the bricks are raised to a height of 6.0 m.

a   Calculate the work done by the crane in lifting the bricks.

....

b   Calculate the energy that has been transferred to the bricks by the crane.

....

c   Name this energy store.

....

4 The girl in Figure 8.4 lifts a heavy box above her head to place it on a shelf.

Figure 8.4: A girl lifting a heavy box over her head to place it on to a shelf.

- Her lifting force is 120 N.
- She lifts the box to a height of 1.6 m.

a Calculate the work done by the girl in lifting the box.

....

....

b The girl decided to push the box up a sloping ramp. State and explain the factors that affect the amount of work she will do pushing up the slope.

....

....

....

....

....

c Explain why pushing the box up the slope might be preferable.

....

....

....

....

....

Challenge

5   We often use machines to allow us to do tasks more easily (for example, a lever to move a heavy object, or a jack to lift a car to change a tyre). This allows us to use a smaller force to do the same work. By considering the conservation of energy, state and explain what else must change, when the force is reduced.

....

....

....

....

....

Figure 8.5: Using a jack to lift a car to change a tyre.

> Power

KEY WORD

watt (W): the SI unit of power; the power when 1 J of work is done in 1 s

KEY EQUATIONS

$$power = \frac{work\ done}{time\ taken} = \frac{W}{t}$$

$$power = \frac{energy\ transferred}{time\ taken} = \frac{\Delta E}{t}$$

> **TIP**
>
> Think of power as the rate of transfer of energy. That way you won't talk about 'power per second' for example, which makes no sense.
>
> Remember that energy isn't created, just transferred. Physicists get upset when you talk about creating energy.

Exercise 8.3

IN THIS EXERCISE YOU WILL:

- check your understanding of the concept of power
- practise calculations involving power.

Focus

1   A light bulb is labelled with its power rating: 60 watt (W).

   a   How many joules of energy does it transfer in 1 s?   ....

   b   How many joules of energy does it transfer in 1 minute?   ....

   c   Why would it be incorrect to say that the bulb supplies 60 J of light each second?

   ....

   ....

   ....

   ....

Practice

2   A growing person needs a diet that supplies about 10 MJ of energy per day. Calculate the amount of energy supplied by such a diet each second, and hence the person's average power. Give your answer to the nearest 10 W.

   ....

   ....

   ....

   ....

3 A motor car is travelling at a steady speed of 30 m/s. The engine provides the force needed to oppose the force of air resistance, 1600 N.

a In the space, draw a diagram to show the four forces that act on the car.

b Calculate the work done by the car each second against the force of air resistance.

....

....

....

....

c What power is supplied by the car's engine? ....

Challenge

4 The air resistance, F_d on a car is related to the speed, v, by the formula

$F_d = kv^2$ (this equation is not in the syllabus).

For a certain car, the value of $k = 0.34$ and the maximum power is 317 kW.

a Calculate the theoretical top speed of this car.

....

....

....

b The actual top speed is actually 78 m/s. State what else might account for the difference.

....

PEER ASSESSMENT

Create a set a set of flash cards for this chapter. Once you've made them, exchange cards with another person and compare theirs to yours. Did you miss anything? Did they?

> Chapter 9

The kinetic model of matter

> States of matter

KEY WORDS

molecular model of matter: a model in which matter consists of molecules in motion

Exercise 9.1

IN THIS EXERCISE YOU WILL:

check that you understand the states of matter.

Focus

1 Which states of matter are being described here? Complete the table.

The first example has been done for you.

Description	State or states
occupies a fixed volume	*solid, liquid*
evaporates to become a gas	
takes the shape of its container	
has a fixed volume	
may become a liquid when its temperature changes	

2 Label each arrow in the diagram below to show the name of the change of state.

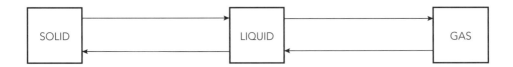

3 **a** State the temperature at which water becomes ice. ....

   b State the temperature at which water boils at standard atmospheric pressure.

   ....

Practice

4 Salt solution freezes at a temperature a few degrees below the freezing point of pure water. You are asked to investigate how the temperature of a salt solution changes as it is cooled from +20 °C to −20 °C. You are provided with an electronic thermometer and a freezer, which is set to give a temperature of −20 °C.

   a Describe how you would set about this task. Draw a diagram if it will help your answer.

   ....

   ....

   ....

   ....

   ....

   ....

   ....

   ....

   ....

   ....

PEER ASSESSMENT

Now compare your answer to that of others. It would be even better if you could trial your own method at home. Have other people made points you could have made? How could you improve your approach?

b On the axes shown, sketch the shape of the temperature–time graph you would expect to obtain. Indicate how you would use the graph to deduce the freezing point of the salt solution.

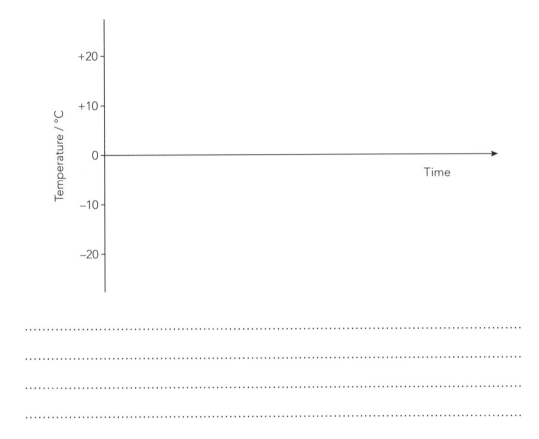

....

....

....

....

Challenge

5 Describe and explain the changes in the molecular structure of water, in the form of ice as it is heated until the water has become steam. Consider

a the arrangement of the molecules

....

....

b the movement of the molecules

....

....

> The kinetic particle model of matter

KEY WORDS

Brownian motion: the motion of microscopic particles suspended in a liquid or gas, caused by molecular bombardment

Exercise 9.2

IN THIS EXERCISE YOU WILL:

- check you understand the model we use to describe matter
- explain the behaviour of matter.

TIP

When talking about the expansion of a solid, liquid or gas, be careful NOT to talk about the particles (atoms/molecules) expanding – they don't.

Focus

1 Complete the table. In the first row, draw sketches of the three states of matter in terms of the arrangement of the particles and their movement. Then describe the three states, referring to the three criteria in the first column.

State	Solid	Liquid	Gas
How close are particles to their neighbours?			
How do the particles move?			
Strength of forces between particles (strong/weak/zero)			

2 a What is the word we use to describe the process of a solid becoming a liquid?

....

b What is the word we use to describe the process of a liquid becoming a gas?

....

c What is the word we use to describe the process of a gas becoming a liquid?

....

Practice

3 Why is this model of matter sometimes described as the 'kinetic' model?

....

....

....

Challenge

4 Why does an aerosol spray feel cold, even on a hot day?

....

....

....

Exercise 9.3

IN THIS EXERCISE YOU WILL:

explore your understanding of the experiment that led us to understand that gases and liquids are made up of molecules.

Figure 9.1 shows the equipment required for observing Brownian motion. The questions in Exercise 9.3 refer to this figure.

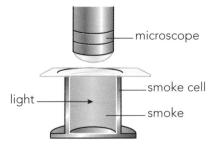

Figure 9.1: The equipment required for observing Browian motion.

Focus

1   On Figure 9.1, show how the light coming from the left reaches the observer looking down the microscope.

2   Explain why a microscope must be used.

....

....

Practice

3   Describe briefly what the observer sees.

....

....

....

4   Explain why we cannot see molecules of air in the smoke cell.

....

....

Challenge

5   Explain the observations briefly using ideas from the particle model of matter.

....

....

....

....

....

> Gases and the kinetic theory

KEY WORDS

absolute (kelvin) scale of temperature (K): the zero of the kelvin scale is absolute zero, the temperature at which all atomic vibration in a solid stops; it is –273 °C.

> **KEY EQUATIONS**
>
> T (in kelvin) = θ (in °C) + 273
>
> ---
>
> pV = constant

> **TIP**
>
> **The gas law equations**
>
> What the equation pV = constant means in practice is that the product of the pressure and volume of a fixed mass of gas always gives you the same answer, as long as the temperature remains the same. So if the gas has pressure = P_1 and volume = V_1 before, and pressure = P_2 and volume = V_2 afterwards, then $P_1V_1 = P_2V_2$, if no change in temperature has occurred.

Exercise 9.4

IN THIS EXERCISE YOU WILL:

describe how the particle model explains the behaviour of gases.

Focus

1   Figure 9.2 represents the particles of a gas inside two containers of the same size. The container on the right (B) has twice as many particles as the one on the left (A), and is at the same temperature.

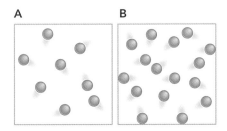

A   B

Figure 9.2: Gas particles inside two containers of the same size.

a   Explain why a gas exerts pressure on the walls of its container using diagram A.

....

....

....

b   State how the density of the gas in B compares to the density of the gas in A.

....

c   Explain why the pressure of the gas in B is greater than that of the gas in A.

....

....

....

d   Describe how you could increase the average speed of the particles in either container.

....

....

....

Practice

2   Look at Figure 9.3. State **two** changes you could make to A to increase its pressure to be the same as B.

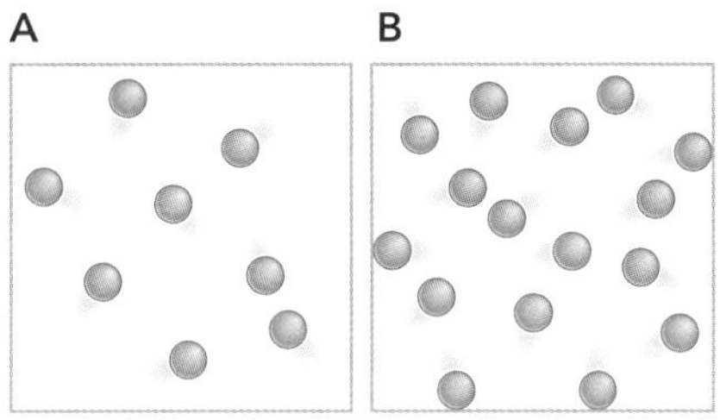

Figure 9.3: Gas molecules inside two containers of the same size.

....

....

....

....

Challenge

3   A sealed container of gas is heated for a long time. After this, the gas is allowed to expand freely. State how the pressure at the end will compare to the pressure at the start. Explain your answer.

....

....

4 Explain why collisions between gas molecules and the container creates pressure.

....

....

....

....

5 Explain why increasing the temperature of a gas increases the pressure it exerts.

....

....

....

....

Exercise 9.5

IN THIS EXERCISE YOU WILL:

check you remember and use laws which govern and predict the large-scale properties (pressure, volume, temperature) of gases.

Focus

1 **a** State the equation that connects pressure and volume of a fixed mass of gas at constant temperature.

....

b Complete the table to show the meanings of the symbols in this equation and their units.

Symbol	Name of quantity	SI unit (name and symbol)
p		
V		

2 What would happen to the pressure of a gas if it was squeezed into a smaller volume?

....

Practice

3   A cylinder contains $400\,cm^3$ of air at a pressure of $2.0 \times 10^5\,Pa$. The air is compressed to a volume of $160\,cm^3$.

Calculate the pressure when the air has returned to its original temperature.

....

....

....

4   In an experiment to investigate the relationship between the pressure and the volume of a fixed mass of gas at constant temperature, a learner obtained the values of pressure and volume shown in the table. Unfortunately, although the learner planned to record five values, they only recorded three.

Pressure of gas / kPa	Volume of gas / cm³	Pressure × volume
100	88	
120		
140	63	
160		
180	50	

a   Calculate the three values for pressure × volume and add them to the third column.

b   Plot these three points on the graph, and draw a suitable curve through them.

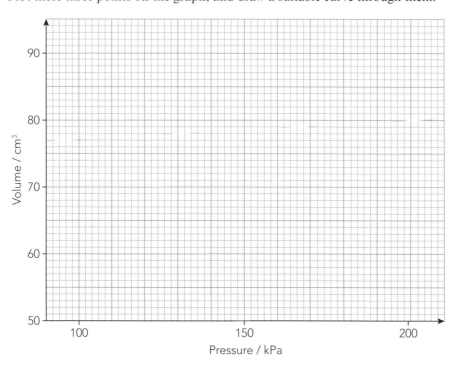

> **TIP**
>
> There are **two** methods you can use to estimate the two missing values for the volume of the gas:
>
> **Method 1:** on the graph, indicate how you would deduce the missing values.
>
> **Method 2:** using the table, deduce the missing values by assuming that Boyle's law is obeyed ($p \times V$ = constant). Write these values in the table.

Challenge

5   Compressing a gas generally increases its temperature. If the pressure of the air in Question **2** had been measured before it had returned to its original temperature, state whether it have been greater than or less than your calculated value. Explain your answer.

....

....

....

Exercise 9.6

IN THIS EXERCISE YOU WILL:

extend your work from Exercise 9.5 to include other laws.

Focus

1   Sketch a graph to show the relationship between the pressure of a gas and its absolute temperature.

Practice

2   A mass of gas is at 20 °C and a pressure of 800 kPa. The gas is heated by putting the container in fire, where the temperature is 500 °C.

    a   State the effect of this change on the pressure of the gas.

    ....

    ....

    ....

    b   If this was an aerosol (for example a deodorant can), why might this change of pressure be concerning?

    ....

    ....

    ....

3   A mass of gas is at 40 °C and a pressure of 200 kPa. It occupies a volume of 100 cm^3. The gas is compressed slowly, so that the temperature does not change.

    a   State what happens to the pressure of the gas

    ....

    ....

    ....

    b   Explain, using the idea of particle movement why the pressure changes in this way

    ....

    ....

    ....

4   A mass of gas is at 40 °C and a pressure of 200 kPa occupies a volume of 100 cm^3. The gas is compressed slowly, so that the temperature does not change. Calculate the new volume when the pressure is 500 kPa.

    ....

    ....

    ....

Challenge

5   a   Create a graph using the data given below. Use the graph to find the value of absolute zero.

Temperature / °C	Pressure / kPa
200	3.93
150	3.52
100	3.10
50	2.68
0	2.27
−50	1.85
−100	1.44
−150	1.02

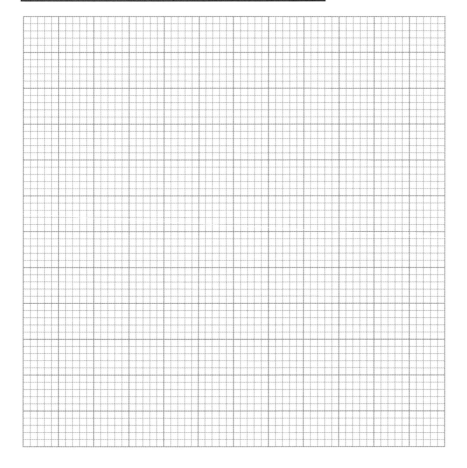

   b   Explain the significance of this temperature.

   ....

   ....

> Chapter 10
Thermal properties of matter

> Temperature, temperature scales and thermal expansion

KEY WORDS

internal energy: the energy of an object; the total kinetic and potential energies of its particles

temperature: a measure of the average kinetic energy of the particles of a substance

Exercise 10.1

IN THIS EXERCISE YOU WILL:

check that you understand the concepts of internal energy and temperature and how they change as a substance changes state.

TIP

Take care not to confuse heat and temperature. Heat refers to the amount of energy possessed by the object, whilst temperature is a measure of the average kinetic energy of the particles in the object. For example, the North Atlantic Drift is a flow of water in the Atlantic Ocean that keeps the UK warmer than it would otherwise be, but it is only at about 8 °C. However, because it is a VERY large volume of water, it has a lot of heat (thermal energy), so it keeps an entire country warmer.

Focus

1   What is internal energy?

    ....

2 Complete the table by writing the correct terms from the list in the spaces in the second column. You will have to use each term more than once.

temperature   thermal energy   internal energy

Statement	Term or terms
increases when an object is supplied with thermal energy	
a measure of the heat of an object	
energy moving from where the temperature is higher to where it is lower	
the sum of all energies of the particles of an object	
a measure of the average kinetic energy of the particles of an object	
tends to spread out from a hot object	
measured using a thermometer	

3 Compare the internal energy possessed by 1 kg of water at 100 °C and 1 kg of steam at 100 °C.

....

....

....

Practice

4 State how you could increase the internal energy of a liquid.

....

5 Explain why steam will give a much worse burn than the same volume of water at the same temperature.

....

....

Challenge

6 Explain why squeezing a gas leads to a rise in temperature.

....

....

....

....

....

7   Figure 10.1 shows a sparkler. The sparks are burning iron filings, at a temperature of 1000 °C. Explain why these can land on your hand without causing injury, but the steel rod the sparkler is mounted on will burn you very badly if you touch it before it has cooled, despite being at a lower temperature.

Figure 10.1: A lit sparkler.

....

....

....

....

....

> Specific heat capacity and changes of state

> ## KEY WORD
>
> **specific heat capacity (c):** the energy required per kilogram and per degree Celsius to raise the temperature of a substance

> ## KEY EQUATION
>
> specific heat capacity = energy required per unit mass per unit temperature increase
>
> $$c = \frac{\Delta E}{m\Delta\theta}$$

> ## TIP
>
> There are two things that tend to cause errors in these calculations:
>
> - not converting units (kW to W, MJ to J, hours to seconds, for example)
>
> - forgetting, or incorrectly writing, the units of specific heat capacity (J/kg °C).
>
> Taking care with these (and generally with the re-arrangement of equations), will mean you do not make the mistakes made by many learners.

Exercise 10.2

> ### IN THIS EXERCISE YOU WILL:
>
> > describe the procedures for calculating the specific heat capacity of a metal
>
> > explain why we take the steps we do during the experiment.

Focus

1   List the equipment necessary to calculate the specific heat capacity of a metal.

....

....

....

....

....

Practice

2   Write a set of instructions to allow someone to accurately calculate the specific heat capacity of a metal.

....

....

....

....

....

Challenge

3   List the improvements that could be made in the following method and state the effect on the result of not making the improvement.

A block of steel is heated to 45 °C using a Bunsen burner. The amount of gas used and the energy density of the gas were noted and the energy supplied calculated. The specific heat capacity was then calculated.

....

....

....

....

....

....

....

....

Exercise 10.3

IN THIS EXERCISE YOU WILL:

- describe changes of state
- describe the factors that can affect the speed of changes of state.

Focus

1   a   State the temperature at which pure ice melts.

....

....

b State the temperature at which pure water boils at standard atmospheric pressure.

....

....

2 State the factors that affect the rate of evaporation.

....

....

....

....

....

....

Practice

3

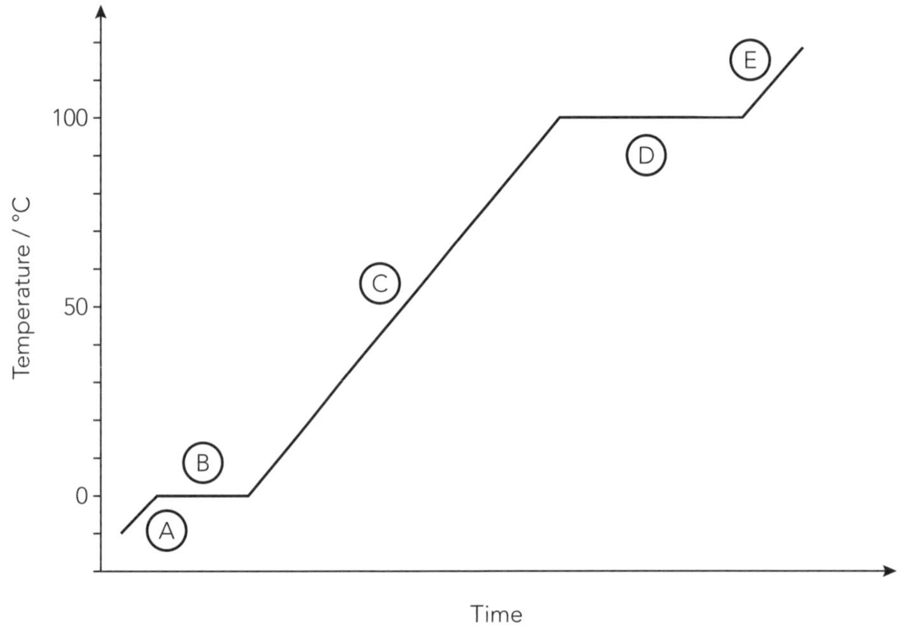

Figure 10.2: A graph of temperature against time for ice being heated at a constant rate.

The graph in Figure 10.2 is obtained from ice being heated at a constant rate in an insulated container. State what is happening at the following positions:

a position B

....

b position D.

....

4   What effect does evaporation have on the temperature of a liquid?

....

5   Explain the difference between evaporation and boiling.

....

....

Challenge

6   Explain, in terms of the arrangement of water molecules, the following processes:

   a   condensation

....

....

   b   solidification.

....

....

7   It is said that a way to cool a bottle of milk is to make the outside surface wet and leave it in a breeze. Explain why this should work.

....

....

....

....

SELF-ASSESSMENT

Consider your answer. Can you pick out the key words that should be used to describe the processes involved? Could you improve your answer?

Exercise 10.4

IN THIS EXERCISE YOU WILL:

> check that you remember the relationship for specific heat capacity

> apply the relationship for specific heat capacity to different situations.

Focus

1 State the equation for calculating the specific heat capacity of a substance.

....

Practice

Table 10.1 shows the specific heat capacities of a variety of materials. Use this information to answer the questions that follow.

Type of material	Material	Specific heat capacity / J/kg°C
metal	steel	420
	aluminium	910
	copper	385
	gold	300
	lead	130
non-metal	glass	670
	nylon	1700
	polythene	2300
	ice	2100
liquid	water	4200
	sea water	3900
	ethanol	2500
	olive oil	1970
gas	air	1000
	water vapour	2020 (at 100 °C)
	methane	2200

Table 10.1: Specific heat capacities of important materials.

2 State which of the metals shown in the table will require the greatest amount of energy to raise the temperature of 100 g from room temperature to 200 °C.

....

3   You have two identical glass beakers containing equal amounts of water and sea water. You heat them using identical electrical heaters, and record their temperatures as they rise. State which temperature will rise more quickly. Explain your answer.

....

....

....

4   A 1.0 kg block of steel is heated in an oven to a temperature of 200 °C. It is then dropped into a tank containing 100 kg of water.

The experiment is then repeated using a 1.0 kg block of aluminium.

State which metal block will cause a bigger rise in the temperature of the water. Explain your answer.

....

....

....

....

5   State which of the following statements are true and which are false. Use the information given in Table 10.1 to arrive at your answer.

Statement	True or false?
All metals have a lower specific heat capacity than all non-metals.	
Metals generally have a lower specific heat capacity than non-metals.	
The specific heat capacity of water decreases when it freezes.	
The specific heat capacity of water decreases when it boils.	

6   Calculate how much energy must be supplied to a 5.0 kg block of copper to increase its temperature from 20 °C to 100 °C.

....

....

7   In an experiment to determine the specific heat capacity of lead, a 0.80 kg block of lead is heated using a 60 W electric heater for 5.0 minutes. Calculate the energy supplied by the heater in this time.

....

....

....

8 **a** The temperature of the block is found to have increased from 20 °C to 165 °C. Use this information to estimate the specific heat capacity of lead.

....

....

b The value you obtain should be higher than that given in Table 10.1. Suggest **two** reasons why this might be.

....

....

9 Sometimes we use materials to store thermal energy. State which of the materials in Table 10.1 would be the best for this.

....

10 If the temperature rise of 1000 kg of water had to be limited to 80 °C, calculate how much energy it could store.

....

....

....

Challenge

11 **a** Storage heaters are sometimes used to store thermal energy supplied by electrical heating. They contain a 100 kg block of concrete, which can rise in temperature by 60 °C above room temperature. If the specific heat capacity of concrete is 1000 J/kg °C, calculate how much energy it stores.

....

....

....

....

....

b Explain why you think concrete is used, rather than water.

....

....

....

....

> Chapter 11
Thermal energy transfers

> Conduction

KEY WORDS

conductor: a substance that transmits thermal energy

insulator: a substance that transmits thermal energy very poorly

conduction: the transfer of thermal energy or electricity through a material without the material itself moving

Exercise 11.1

IN THIS EXERCISE YOU WILL:

- describe examples of conductors and insulators
- explain experimental approaches to comparing thermal conductivities
- > check your understanding of why some materials are good thermal (and electrical) conductors.

Focus

1   a   Copper is an example of a good conductor of thermal energy.

   What word is the opposite of 'conductor'? ....

   b   Give another example of a good conductor of thermal energy. ....

   c   Give an example of a bad conductor of thermal energy. ....

2   State what metals have that non-metals generally do not have which allows better thermal and electrical conduction.

   ....

   ....

   ....

Practice

3 Figure 11.1 shows an experiment used to compare different metals.

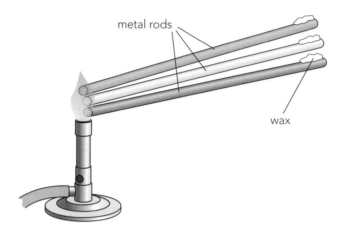

Figure 11.1: Three rods of different metals, with one end of each being heated, and solid wax on the other end.

    a State **two** things that must be the same for all three rods if this is to be a fair test.

....

....

    b Explain how you can tell which metal is the best conductor, and which is the worst.

....

....

....

4 Metals are usually good conductors of both thermal energy and electricity. Explain why this is.

....

....

....

....

Challenge

5 The experiment described in Question **3** is NOT a very good fair test. Suppose that two rods were equally good conductors, but one had a very small specific heat capacity while the other had a very high specific heat capacity. State on which the wax would melt first. Explain your answer.

....

....

....

....

6 Explain why liquids and gases are poor conductors of thermal energy.

....

....

....

> Convection

KEY WORD

convection: the transfer of thermal energy through a material by movement of the material itself

Exercise 11.2

IN THIS EXERCISE YOU WILL:

- check that you recall and understand what convection is
- describe how convection works
- describe practical implications of convection as thermal energy transfer.

Focus

1 Explain what convection is.

....

....

....

Practice

2 a Figure 11.2 shows a room with a heater next to one wall, opposite a window. Draw on the
diagram to show how a convection current will form in the room when the heater is switched on.

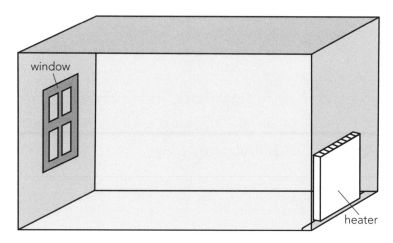

Figure 11.2: A room with a heater next to one wall, opposite a window.

   b Explain, in terms of convection, why it would not be sensible to fix the heater high up on
the wall, close to the ceiling.

   ....

   ....

   ....

3 How do the following quantities change when air is heated? Choose from:

increases   decreases   stays the same

   a Temperature ....   **b** Mass ....

   c Density ....   **d** Separation of molecules ....

   e Speed of molecules ....

Challenge

4 Explain in detail why the smoke produced by a candle flame rises upwards.

   ....

   ....

   ....

   ....

   ....

   ....

> Radiation

KEY WORDS

infrared radiation: electromagnetic radiation whose wavelength is greater than that of visible light; sometimes known as thermal radiation

electromagnetic radiation: energy travelling in the form of waves

TIP

In physics, we talk about two kinds of radiation – ionising and non-ionising. Most of the electromagnetic spectrum isn't ionising – the exceptions are X-rays and gamma rays. Nuclear radiation is ionising. (See Chapter 22.) Make sure you are clear on the difference.

Exercise 11.3

IN THIS EXERCISE YOU WILL:

- check your understanding of what infrared radiation (IR) is
- explain how different surfaces emit, absorb and reflect IR, and describe practical implications of this mechanism of thermal energy transfer
- check your understanding of the different factors affecting the rate of transfer of IR.

Focus

1   State what thermal (or infrared) radiation is.

   ....

   ....

   ....

   ....

2   Two identical cups containing equal volumes of water sit on a table. One starts at a temperature of 50 °C and the other at 40 °C. State which will cool fastest. Explain your answer.

   ....

   ....

   ....

   ....

   ....

Practice

3 Explain why energy can reach us from the Sun by radiation but not by conduction or convection.

....

....

....

4 Infrared radiation may be absorbed when it reaches the surface of an object. Describe the surface of an object that is a good absorber of infrared radiation.

....

....

5 What effect does infrared radiation have on an object that absorbs it?

....

....

6 Explain why a cold object warms up and a warm object cools in the same room at the same time, in terms of exchange of infrared radiation.

....

....

....

7 An ice cube taken from the freezer will rise in temperature, but when it reaches room temperature, it will remain at this temperature. Explain why this happens.

....

....

....

Challenge

> **TIP**
>
> Insulation is all about reducing thermal energy transfer. We can't stop it, so don't be tempted to say 'insulation stops heat loss'. To be as effective as possible, what we do needs to address every means of thermal energy transfer. Remember, if it stops thermal energy leaving, it will also stop thermal energy getting in.

8 In cold countries, windows are often fitted with double glazing. This consists of two sheets of glass separated by a gap a few millimetres wide. There is usually a vacuum in the gap.

a   Explain why very little energy escapes from the room by conduction.

....

....

....

b   Explain why very little energy can escape from the room by convection.

....

....

....

c   Can energy escape by radiation? Explain your answer.

....

....

....

9   A television remote control uses infrared radiation to send instructions to the TV set. If you point it in the opposite direction, the beam misses the TV set and nothing happens.

However, infrared radiation can be reflected by hard, shiny surfaces such as glass or aluminium. In the space below, draw a diagram to show how you could use a remote control, a TV set and a sheet of aluminium to show the reflection of infrared radiation. (You may be able to try this experiment at home: use a large china plate instead of the metal sheet.)

Try this at home: Although our eyes cannot see infrared radiation, a digital camera may detect it. Try shining a TV remote control into a digital camera. Can you see the camera light up when you press the buttons on the TV remote control?

10 Imagine you've just made a cup of coffee when someone phones you. You know this conversation will take some time. Using your knowledge of thermal radiation and specific heat capacity, decide, and then explain, whether you should put your milk in before you answer the phone or after, so that the coffee is hottest when you drink it.

....

....

....

11 The heat sink around the processor in a computer is often piece of aluminium. It is needed to remove thermal energy from the processor whilst the processor is in operation. State and explain two design features that would make it an effective emitter of thermal radiation, to allow the processor to remain cool enough to function properly.

....

....

....

....

....

12 Explain why gases such as carbon dioxide and methane produce global warming.

....

....

....

....

....

> Some consequences of thermal energy transfer

Exercise 11.4

IN THIS EXERCISE YOU WILL:

- check that you understand experimental technique, in the context of thermal energy transfer
- explain how a vacuum flask works.

Focus

1   Figure 11.3 shows an experiment to investigate the loss of energy from a beaker of hot water. Beaker A has a plastic lid; beaker B has no lid.

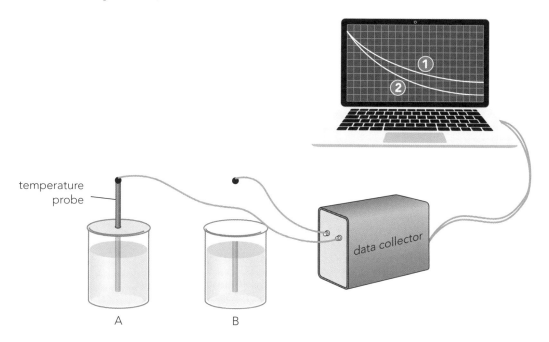

Figure 11.3: An experiment to investigate the loss of energy from a beaker of hot water, with and without a lid.

At the start of the experiment, both beakers are filled with hot water from a kettle. The temperature sensors record the changing temperature of the water in each beaker.

a   State **one** quantity that should be the same for each beaker if this is to be a fair test.

   ....

b   State **one** other factor that should be controlled if this is to be a fair test.

   ....

c   State which graph line (1 or 2) on the image of the computer in Figure 11.3 is for beaker A.

   ....

d   Explain your answer.

   ....

Practice

2   It is suggested that beaker B in Figure 11.3 is losing energy by convection. State in what other way it could be losing energy.

   ....

3 Explain why it would have been a fairer test if the beakers had been insulated around their sides and bases.

....

....

Challenge

4 Figure 11.4 shows a vacuum flask, which is very good at reducing the transfer of thermal energy into or out of the contents, which are put inside the flask. Use your knowledge of the ways that thermal energy transfer occurs to explain how the flask is effective.

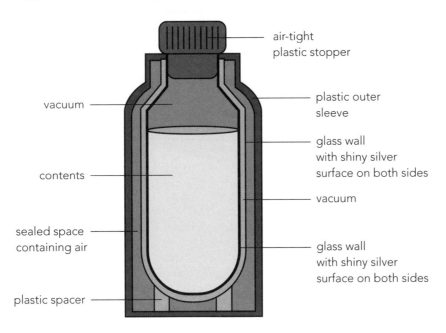

Figure 11.4: The structure of a vacuum flask.

....

....

....

....

....

....

....

....

....

....

....

....

....

....

....

....

PEER ASSESSMENT

Compare your answer to those of others. It is important to have considered each aspect of the design and the contribution it makes to the flask's effectiveness. How did you do?

 # Exercise 11.5

IN THIS EXERCISE YOU WILL:

> apply your knowledge to the Earth and how it gains and loses thermal energy.

The Earth is a giant rock in space. It is about 150 million kilometres from the Sun. It is daytime on the side of the Earth facing the Sun. It is night-time on the other side (see Figure 11.5).

Sun   Earth

Figure 11.5: The relative positions of the Earth and the Sun, and where day and night are on the Earth as a result.

The Earth's average temperature is about 15 °C. The Earth is in space. Space is very cold, with its temperature being about −270 °C. Because the Earth is warmer than space, it is constantly losing energy into space.

Focus

1   State how the Earth transfers energy into space: by conduction, by convection or by radiation.

....

2   Describe what would happen to the temperature of the Earth if the Sun stopped shining.

....

....

3   Fortunately, the Sun shines at an almost steady rate. The side of the Earth facing the Sun absorbs the Sun's radiation.

    a   Name the **three** types of electromagnetic radiation that reach the Earth from the Sun.

....

....

....

    b   Explain what happens to the temperature of the Earth on the side facing the Sun.

....

....

Practice

4   Explain why the temperature of the Earth usually falls at night.

....

....

....

5   Because the Earth spins on its axis, the night ends and a new day begins. The graph in Figure 11.6 shows how the temperature at a point on the Earth varies during a week.

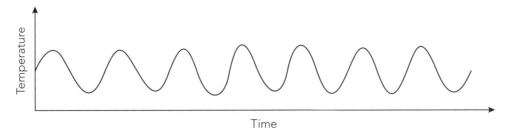

Figure 11.6: Graph of the variation of temperature at a point on the Earth's surface over the period of one week.

Explain why the lowest temperature is often just before dawn.

....

....

....

Challenge

6 Imagine that the Earth turned more slowly, so that a day lasted twice as long: 48 hours. Think about temperatures during the day and at night. Describe the changes that we would notice. Explain your answer. Illustrate your answer with a graph similar to the one in Figure 11.6.

....

....

....

Chapter 12

Sound

> Making sounds and the speed of sound

KEY WORD

pitch: how high or low a note sounds

Exercise 12.1

IN THIS EXERCISE YOU WILL:

- check that you understand how sound is made
- practise remembering the normal human hearing range
- practise measuring the speed of sound
- use the wave equation (see Chapter 14).

Focus

1 **a** State the one word that describes the movement of a source of sound.

....

b State which part of a guitar moves to produce a sound.

....

c State what moves when a wind instrument such as a flute produces a sound.

....

d State what we call a reflected sound.

....

2 State the speed of sound in air.

....

3 State the normal hearing range for humans.

....

Practice

4 Arun can hear sounds with frequencies up to 20 kHz. His grandfather cannot hear sounds above 12 kHz.

Which **two** of the following sound frequencies will Arun hear but his grandfather will not?

8.0 kHz   25.2 kHz   16.5 kHz   14.9 kHz   11.8 kHz

....

5 You can probably hear notes of higher pitch than your teacher. Describe how you would show this in the school laboratory.

....

....

....

....

....

6 a Calculate how long a sound will take to travel 1 km in air. Give your answer in seconds, to one decimal place.

....

....

....

b Calculate how far sound will travel in 5 s in air.

....

....

7 Figure 12.1 shows a method for determining the speed of sound.

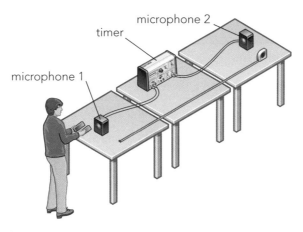

Figure 12.1: A method for calculating the speed of sound.

Complete the following sentences:

a This experiment measures the speed of sound in ....

b To make a sound ....

....

c The microphones detect the sound and the timer shows ....

....

d The boy must also measure ....

....

e The formula for calculating the speed of sound from this experiment is ....

> **TIP**
>
> Make sure you know how to convert between units – milliseconds to seconds, kilometres to metres, etc. – as these are common in this section.

Challenge

8 In an experiment to measure the speed of sound in glass, a pulse of sound is sent into a glass rod, 14.0 m in length. The reflected sound is detected after 5.6 ms (0.0056 s). Calculate the speed of sound in glass.

....

....

....

> Seeing sounds

> **KEY WORDS**
>
> **amplitude:** the greatest height of a wave above its undisturbed level
>
> **period:** the time for one complete vibration or the passage of one complete wave
>
> **frequency:** the number of vibrations per second or waves per second passing a point
>
> **ultrasound:** sound waves whose frequency is so high that they cannot be heard
>
> **compression:** a region of a sound wave where the particles are pushed close together
>
> **rarefaction:** a region of a sound wave where the particles are further apart

Exercise 12.2

IN THIS EXERCISE YOU WILL:

- practise remembering the key words associated with waves and label a diagram with them
- relate wave and sound properties.

Focus

You might like to refer to Chapter 14, 'Properties of waves', of the Coursebook at this point.

1 **a** State what kind of wave sound is.

....

   b State which kind of seismic wave is the same type of wave as sound.

....

   c State what characterises this kind of wave has.

....

Practice

2 Figure 12.2 shows a trace that represents a sound wave. Add labelled arrows to the diagram to show the amplitude *A* of the wave and its period *T*.

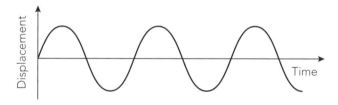

Figure 12.2: A graph of displacement against time representing a sound wave.

3 Figure 12.3 shows a trace that represents a sound wave. Draw on the diagram to show a second wave that has the same pitch but is louder.

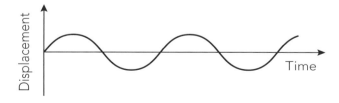

Figure 12.3: A graph of displacement against time representing a sound wave.

4   Two sound waves have the frequencies shown:

- sound A, 440 Hz

- sound B, 520 Hz.

a   State which sound has the higher pitch. ....

b   Calculate the period of sound A.

....

....

Challenge

5   Draw a table which shows the connection between the properties of a sound and the properties of the wave causing the sound.

TIP

Make sure you don't confuse wave properties with sound properties.

Exercise 12.3

IN THIS EXERCISE YOU WILL:

- compare sound to other waves
- explain how to use some laboratory equipment used to make measurements for sound waves
- recall the definition of ultrasound.

Focus

1   State which has the higher frequency – ultrasound or an opera singer's voice.

....

Practice

2 Can sound waves travel through a vacuum (empty space)? ....

3 **a** State what instrument we use to detect sound waves in the school laboratory. ....

    b State what instrument do we use to display sound waves on a screen. ....

Challenge

4 A drummer strikes the horizontal surface of a drum so that a sound wave travels upwards from the surface of the drum. Describe how a molecule of the air above the drum will move as the sound wave travels upwards. It may help to include a simple diagram.

....

....

....

....

Exercise 12.4

IN THIS EXERCISE YOU WILL:

> look at sound waves and ultrasound in more detail

> consider the benefits of digital transmission of sound.

Focus

1 Complete the following sentences, using words from the list below. Each word may be used once, more than once, or not at all:

    compressions   longitudinal   high   transverse   rarefaction

    low   electromagnetic   peaks   atmospheric   troughs

Sound waves are .... waves. They consist of ...., which are

.... pressure areas and ...., which are ....

pressure areas.

Practice

2   State three uses of ultrasound and for each, give a brief description of how it is useful.

....

....

....

....

....

....

3   In the 1980s the use of magnetic cassette tapes became widespread to store music. Today, music is stored on phones or streamed through an app. Apart from the storage device, state the other fundamental difference between the music stored on a cassette and that stored on a phone.

....

....

....

Challenge

4   Describe the benefits in transmitting and storing signals in this form.

....

....

....

....

....

....

....

....

....

....

PEER ASSESSMENT

Compare your thoughts with those of others. Can you think of any disadvantages of digital for transmission and for storage?

Chapter 13

Light

> Reflecting light

KEY WORDS

ray diagram: a diagram showing the paths of typical rays of light

real image: an image that can be formed on a screen

virtual image: an image that cannot be formed on a screen; it is formed when rays of light appear to be spreading out from a point

reflection: the change in direction of a ray of light when it strikes a surface without passing through it

angle of reflection: the angle between the reflected ray and the normal

plane (mirror): plane means 'flat', so a plane mirror is a flat mirror

normal: means 'at 90° to'; a normal is a line at 90° to a surface (for example, the surface of a mirror) or boundary between two materials (for example, the boundary between air and glass)

Exercise 13.1

IN THIS EXERCISE YOU WILL:

- practise drawing ray diagrams
- check your understanding of real and virtual images

> use ray diagrams to predict where an image will be formed.

Focus

1 State the kind of image is formed in a mirror.

   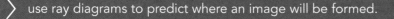

2 State the property of the reflection that means an image cannot be formed on a screen.

   ....

3 If the angle a ray of light makes with the mirror is 22°, calculate its angle of reflection. State the relationship that allows you to say what the angle will be.

   ....

4 The incomplete ray diagram in Figure 13.1 shows an object in front of a plane mirror. Three light rays are shown leaving the object.

    a Follow the instructions to complete the diagram.

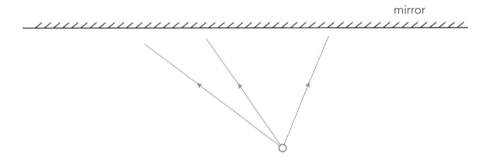

Figure 13.1: An incomplete ray diagram for an object in front of a plane mirror.

- Extend the rays to the mirror.
- For each ray, use a ruler and protractor to draw the reflected rays.
- Extend the reflected rays to find where they meet.
- Mark the position of the image.
- Measure how far the image is from the mirror.

    b State the distance of the image from the mirror. •••

    c Is this image real or virtual? ....

    d Explain how you know.

       ....

       ....

Practice

5 Figure 13.2 shows a ray of light incident on a pair of mirrors.

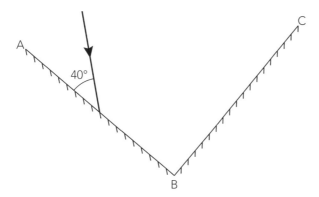

Figure 13.2: A ray of light striking two plane mirrors at right angles to each other.

a Draw the path of the light as it reflects from mirror **AB**.

b Draw the path of this light from mirror **BC**.

c Complete this sentence. The incident and final reflected rays are ....

....

Challenge

6 Determine how long a mirror has to be for you to see your whole reflection.

> **TIP**
>
> Draw a diagram. Consider a ray from the feet going to bottom of the mirror and then reflected back to the eyes, and a ray from the top of the head travelling almost horizontally to the top of the mirror. Then consider the geometry of the rays.

....

....

> Refraction of light

KEY WORDS

refraction: the bending of a ray of light on passing from one material to another

speed of light: the speed at which light travels; this is 3.0×10^8 m/s in a vacuum

normal: means 'at 90° to'; a normal is a line at 90° to a surface (for example, the surface of a mirror) or boundary between two materials (for example, the boundary between air and glass)

angle of incidence: the angle between the incident ray and the normal

angle of refraction: the angle between the refracted ray and the normal

refractive index: the ratio of the speeds of a wave in two different regions

KEY EQUATIONS

$$\text{refractive index} = \frac{\text{sin angle of incidence}}{\text{sin angle of refraction}}$$

$$n = \frac{\sin i}{\sin r}$$

$$\text{refractive index} = \frac{1}{\text{sin angle of refraction}}$$

$$n = \frac{1}{\sin c}$$

Exercise 13.2

IN THIS EXERCISE YOU WILL:

- complete a diagram to show that a ray of light is refracted when it passes from one transparent material to another
- explain how light behaves when refracted and the effect of refraction on the direction and speed of light.

Focus

1 State what happens to the speed of light when light travels from air into glass.

....

2 State what happens to the speed of light when light travels from air into a vacuum.

....

Practice

3 Figure 13.3 shows a ray of light travelling from air into glass.

a Follow the instructions to complete the diagram.

- Label the materials 'air' and 'glass'.
- Add arrows to the rays to show the direction in which the light is travelling.
- Using a ruler, draw the normal to the surface at the point where the ray enters the glass.
- Add labels 'incident ray' and 'refracted ray'.
- Using a protractor, measure the angles of incidence and refraction.

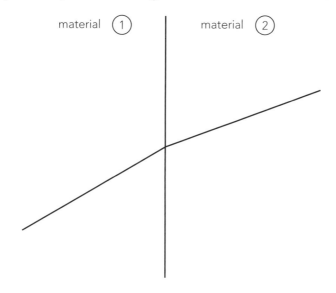

material ①   material ②

Figure 13.3: A ray of light travelling from air into glass.

b Explain how you know which material is air and which is glass.

....

....

....

c State the angle of incidence. ....

d State the angle of refraction. ....

Challenge

4 Sometimes a dry road looks wet on a hot day. This is one effect of refraction.

a Explain why this happens.

....

....

....

....

b How does this effect differ from total internal reflection?

....

....

....

....

Exercise 13.3

IN THIS EXERCISE YOU WILL:

> explain that light travels at different speeds in different materials and this is what causes refraction

> gain confidence in your understanding of refractive index.

Focus

1 The refractive index of a certain material is 1.45. State whether light travels faster or slower in the material than in air.

....

2 A ray of light passes through the material in Question **1**. As it leaves the material, state whether it will bend towards or away from the normal.

....

Practice

3 A ray of light passing through air enters a block of Perspex®. Its angle of incidence is 30°.

   a Draw a diagram of this, showing the angles of incidence and refraction.

   b The refractive index of Perspex® is 1.50. Calculate the speed of light in the glass. Give your answer to one decimal place. The speed of light in air is 3.0×10^8 m/s.

....

....

c   Calculate the angle of refraction on entering the block.

....

4   Explain, using Figure 13.4, why a swimming pool does not look as deep as it actually is.

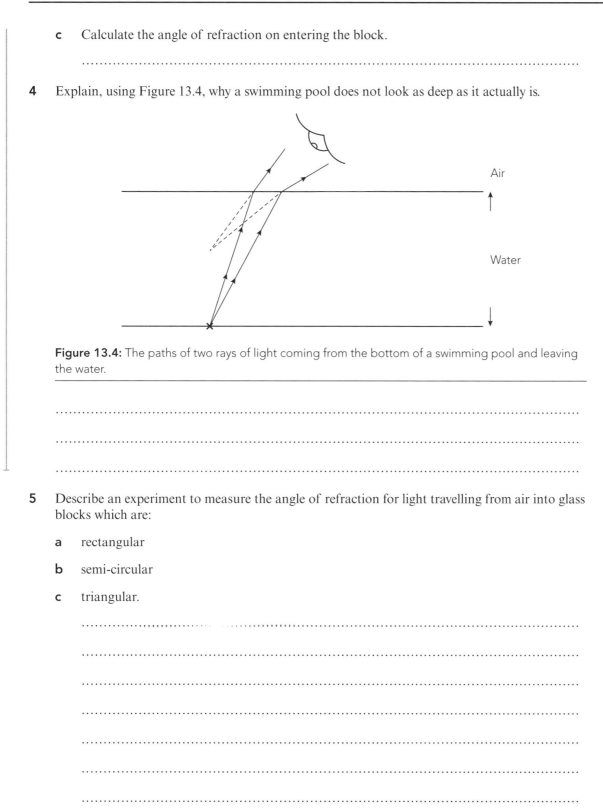

Figure 13.4: The paths of two rays of light coming from the bottom of a swimming pool and leaving the water.

....

....

....

5   Describe an experiment to measure the angle of refraction for light travelling from air into glass blocks which are:

a   rectangular

b   semi-circular

c   triangular.

....

....

....

....

....

....

....

....

d In the case of the triangular block, describe how you would show that white light is made up of different colours and state the spectrum produced, in order of decreasing wavelength.

....

....

....

....

Challenge

6 When light travels between two materials, refraction often occurs. State the property of the materials you would change to increase the effect.

....

TIP

Refraction happens in the atmosphere as waves travel up through it towards space. What is the property of the atmosphere, which changes as you move further from the surface of the Earth, that causes this?

PEER ASSESSMENT

Pair up with a partner and discuss your answers. Try to agree on them! Present your answers to the class, pair-by-pair.

> Total internal reflection

KEY WORDS

total internal reflection: when a ray of light strikes the inner surface of a solid material and 100% of the light reflects back inside it

critical angle: the minimum angle of incidence at which total internal reflection occurs; it has the symbol c

Exercise 13.4

IN THIS EXERCISE YOU WILL:

- recall what happens when light is reflected in the process of total internal reflection
- explain the significance of the critical angle
- describe applications of total internal reflection in the real world.

Focus

1   Triangular prisms are often used as perfect mirrors in periscopes, telescopes and binoculars. Figure 13.5 shows how a light ray is reflected by a prism (the angles of the prism are 90°, 45°, 45°).

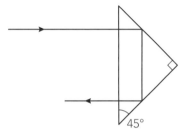

Figure 13.5: How light is totally internally reflected in a triangular prism.

    a   Mark with an X two points at which the light ray undergoes total internal reflection.

    b   State the angle of incidence of the ray at this point. ....

Practice

2   Explain why the ray in Figure 13.5 does not bend at the point where it enters the prism, or where it leaves the prism.

....

....

....

....

3   If light left a swimming pool like this, describe how the real and apparent depths would compare.

....

Challenge

4   Figure 13.6 shows a periscope that makes use of two prisms.

   a   Complete the diagram by extending the two rays until they reach the observer.

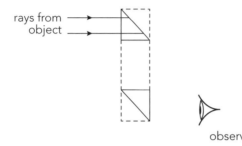

   Figure 13.6: Two triangular prisms, like the one in Figure 13.5, used to make a periscope.

   b   Explain how you can tell from Figure 13.6 that the image seen by the observer will be the right way up, rather than inverted.

   ....

   ....

   ....

   ....

5   Figure 13.7 shows light travelling down an optic fibre. Explain, using the diagram, why it is important that these fibres are not bent too much.

   Figure 13.7: A ray of light passing through an optic fibre.

   ....

   ....

   ....

   ....

> Lenses

KEY WORDS

converging lens: rays entering the lens parallel to the principal axis pass through the principal focus after leaving the lens; these lenses usually form real images

diverging lens: rays entering the lens parallel to the principal axis, diverge as if they came from the principal focus; these lenses form virtual images. Diverge means to get further apart

principal axis: the line passing through the centre of a lens, perpendicular to its surface

principal focus: the point at which rays of light parallel to the axis converge after passing through a converging lens

focal length: the distance between the centre of the lens and the principal focus

Exercise 13.5

IN THIS EXERCISE YOU WILL:

- explain your understanding of lenses
- draw ray diagrams for real images formed by lenses
- describe real-world applications of lenses.

TIP

Converging lenses are everywhere – in cameras, in telescopes, in our eyes. A converging lens collects rays of light and focuses them to form an image. Check that you understand the rules for drawing ray diagrams.

Focus

1 Figure 13.8 shows an incomplete ray diagram – no rays have been drawn yet! There is an object O to the left of the lens.

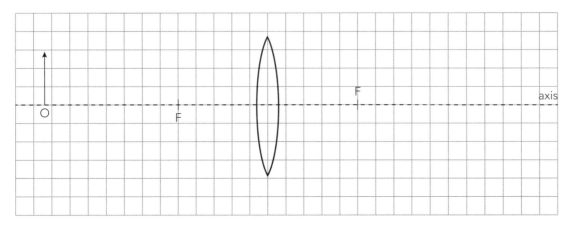

Figure 13.8: An incomplete ray diagram showing an object (O) at a distance greater than twice the focal length of the lens.

a State whether this is a converging or diverging lens. ....

b State how you know this. ....

c State what the letter F indicates. ....

Practice

2 a Complete the ray diagram in Figure 13.8 by following the instructions.

   • Starting at the top of the object, draw one ray passing through the centre of the lens.

   • Again starting from the top of the object, draw a second ray that is initially parallel to the principal axis of the lens.

   • Indicate where the image of the object is formed.

   b State which is bigger, the object or the image. ....

   c State which is further from the lens, the object or the image. ....

   d State whether the image is upright or inverted. ....

3 You can use a ray diagram as a scale drawing.

   a The focal length of the lens is 10.0 cm. State how far the image is from the centre of the

      lens ....

   b The object is 6.0 mm tall. State the size of the image. ....

Challenge

4 When a converging lens is used as a magnifying glass, the object O (marked on the diagram below) must be closer to the lens than F, the focal length.

a Complete the ray diagram in Figure 13.9 to show where the image of O will be formed.

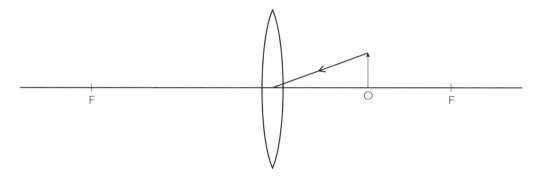

Figure 13.9: A ray diagram showing an object (O) at a distance less than the focal length of the lens.

b State whether the image is upright or inverted. ....

c State whether the image is real or virtual. ....

d Explain how you can tell from the diagram that the image is magnified.

....

....

....

5 State which type of lens is used in eye glasses to correct long sight.

....

> Dispersion of light

KEY WORD

spectrum: waves, or colours of light, separated out in order according to their wavelengths

Exercise 13.6

IN THIS EXERCISE YOU WILL:

recall key facts about light waves and the visible spectrum and their dangers.

Focus

1 The visible spectrum is the spectrum of all the colours of light that we can see.

   a State which colour in the visible spectrum has the shortest wavelength. ....

   b State which colour in the visible spectrum has the highest frequency. ....

   c State which colour comes between green and indigo. ....

   d State which colour has a wavelength longer than orange light. ....

Practice

2 Figure 13.10 represents two waves of visible light, observed for a tiny fraction of a second.

Figure 13.10: Two waves of visible light, observed for a tiny fraction of a second.

   a State which wave (A or B) has the greater wavelength. ....

   b State how many complete waves there are in trace A. ....

   c State how many complete waves there are in trace B. ....

   d   Explain how you can tell that the waves are travelling at the same speed.

   ....

   ....

   e   State which wave represents light of a higher frequency. ....

   f   The waves represent red and violet light. State which one represents red light.

   ....

Challenge

3   Describe an experiment to show the dispersion of white light.

....

....

....

....

....

....

4   Explain what monochromatic means.

....

....

....

....

....

....

> Chapter 14

Properties of waves

> Describing waves

KEY WORDS

transverse wave: a wave in which the vibration is at right angles to the direction in which the wave is travelling

period: the time for one complete oscillation of a pendulum, one complete vibration or the passage of one complete wave

frequency: the number of vibrations per second or waves per second passing a point

longitudinal wave: a wave in which the vibration is forward and back, along the direction in which the wave is travelling

amplitude: the greatest height of a wave above its undisturbed level

wavelength: the distance between adjacent crests (or troughs) of a wave

---

Exercise 14.1

IN THIS EXERCISE YOU WILL:

- recall that a wave transfers energy from place to place without any matter being transferred
- explain that are many different types of wave but they all have certain things in common
- practise your understanding of wave motion
- recall key words for describing the properties of waves.

Focus

1   Figure 14.1 represents a transverse wave in a string. The origin of the axes can be thought of as where the string is being held and shaken by someone.

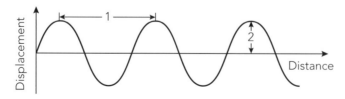

Figure 14.1: A transverse wave in a string.

a   The *y*-axis shows how much the wave is disturbed from its undisturbed level.
State what the *x*-axis shows.

....

b   State what quantity the horizontal arrow 1 indicates. ....

c   State the symbol that is used for this quantity and the units it is measured in. ....

d   State what quantity the vertical arrow 2 indicates. ....

e   State the symbol that is used for this quantity. ....

2   Figure 14.2 represents a wave. This graph has the time *t* on the *x*-axis.

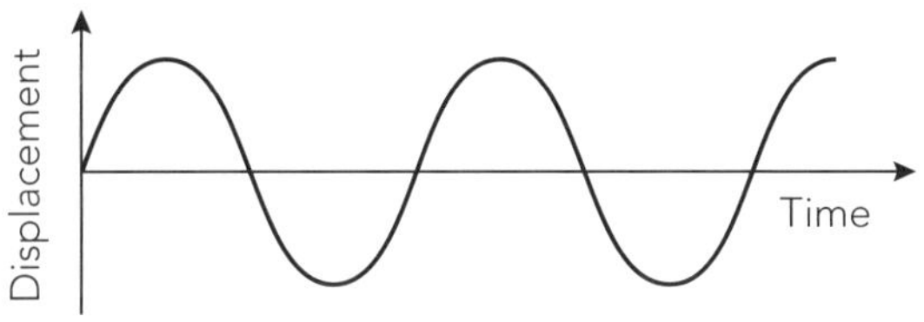

Figure 14.2: A transverse wave in a string.

a   On the graph, add the labels 'crest' and 'trough' in the correct places.

b   Mark a time interval that represents the period *T* of the wave. Label this *T*.

c   The period of the wave is 0.002 s. Calculate its frequency *f*. Be sure to give the correct unit.

....

....

3   Waves can be described as transverse or longitudinal.

a   State in which type of wave the vibrations are at right angles to the direction that the wave

is travelling. ....

b   State which type of wave a sound wave is. ....

c   State which type of wave a light wave is. ....

4   You have a long spring stretched out in front of you on a long table. Another learner holds the
far end so that it cannot move.

a   Describe how you should move your end of the spring to produce a transverse wave.

....

....

b   Describe how you should move your end of the spring to produce a longitudinal wave.

....

....

Practice

5 Without looking at the coursebook, draw and label the following features.

    a A transverse wave (include a horizontal line to show the undisturbed position).

    b A longitudinal wave (you can't really mark on the amplitude or the undisturbed position, but you can label a wavelength).

PEER ASSESSMENT

Use the table provided to indicate your progress.

Draw a 'smiley face' in the second column if you did it really well.

Draw a face with a straight line if you made a good attempt.

Leave the box blank if you did not try to do it, or did not succeed.

Checklist	Assessment
You used a sharp pencil for drawing.	
You drew single clean lines; the lines are not broken or fuzzy.	
You marked on the undisturbed position correctly.	
You marked the wavelength correctly (transverse).	
You marked on the amplitude correctly (transverse).	
You marked the wavelength correctly (longitudinal).	

If you left boxes blank, see Chapter 14: 14.1 'Describing waves' in the coursebook.

Challenge

6   Describe which property of a sound wave changes when a sound gets louder.

> **TIP**
>
> Think about which wave has the most energy or delivers the most power.

....

....

7   Explain how an orchestra illustrates that all sound has the same speed in air.

....

....

〉 Speed, frequency and wavelength

> **KEY WORDS**
>
> **wave equation:** the equation linking wave speed, frequency and wavelength
>
> **wave speed:** the speed at which a wave travels

> **KEY EQUATION**
>
> wave speed = frequency × wavelength
>
> $v = f\lambda$

Exercise 14.2

> **IN THIS EXERCISE YOU WILL:**
>
> - practise calculating the speed of a wave crest as the wave travels along
> - use the wave equation $v = f\lambda$ to show how wave speed (v) is related to frequency (f) and wavelength (λ).

> **TIP**
>
> In these calculations, you are quite likely to come across conversions in units, so make sure you know the meanings of prefixes such as m (milli = 1/1000), k (kilo = 1000) and M (mega = 1 000 000).

Focus

1 Complete the table to show the quantities related by the equation $v = f\lambda$ and their units.

Symbol	Quantity	Unit (name and symbol)
v		
f		
λ		

2 A particular sound wave has a frequency of 100 Hz.

   a State how many waves pass a point in 1 s. ....

   b Each wave has a wavelength of 3.3 m. Calculate the total length of the waves that pass a

   point in 1 s. ....

   c Calculate the speed of the sound wave. ....

Practice

3 Seismic waves are caused by earthquakes. They travel out from the affected area and can be detected around the world. They have low frequencies (mostly too low to hear) and travel at the speed of sound.

   a A particular seismic wave is travelling through granite with a speed of 5000 m/s. Its frequency is 8.0 Hz. Calculate its wavelength.

   ....

   ....

   ....

   b The wave is detected 12.5 minutes after the earthquake. Estimate the distance from the detector to the site of the earthquake.

   ....

   ....

   ....

Challenge

4 Explain why your answer to Question **3b** can only be an estimate.

   ....

5　**a**　Light travels at a speed of 3.0×10^8 m/s. Red light has a wavelength of 7.0×10^{-7} m. Calculate its frequency.

....

....

　　b　Infrared radiation travels at the same speed as light, but it has a lower frequency than red light. State whether its wavelength is greater than or less than that of red light.

....

〉 Explaining wave phenomena

KEY WORDS

wavefront: a line joining adjacent points on a wave that are all in step with each other

diffraction: when a wave spreads out as it travels through a gap or past the edge of an object

Exercise 14.3

IN THIS EXERCISE YOU WILL:

- check your understanding of how waves behave and change during refraction
- check your understanding of diffraction through a gap and at an edge.

Focus

1　Complete the table to show the names of each of these aspects of waves.

TIP

Each word ends in …tion.

Description	Name
bouncing off a surface	
changing direction because of a change of speed	
spreading out after passing through a gap	

Practice

2 Figure 14.3 shows light waves travelling through two different materials, 1 and 2.

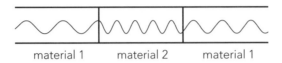

material 1   material 2   material 1

Figure 14.3: Ray diagram of a light wave travelling through two different materials.

Complete the table to show how the speed, wavelength and frequency of the waves change as they travel from material 1 into material 2.

Quantity	Increases / decreases / stays the same
wave speed	
wavelength	
frequency	

3 Figure 14.4 shows wavefronts passing through a gap.

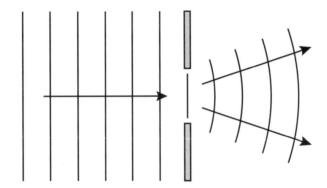

Figure 14.4: Ray diagram for wavefronts passing through a gap.

a On Figure 14.4, mark the wavelength of the waves.

b   In the space below, draw a similar diagram to show waves having the same wavelength passing through a wider gap.

Challenge

4   It is possible to hear a conversation through a partially open door, but not to see the people talking. Explain this using the idea of diffraction.

....

....

....

....

....

Figure 14.5: Diffraction means sometimes you can hear conversations, but you can't see the people who are speaking!

> Chapter 15

The electromagnetic spectrum

KEY WORDS

electromagnetic spectrum: the family of radiations similar to light

ultraviolet radiation: electromagnetic radiation whose frequency is higher than that of visible light

infrared radiation: electromagnetic radiation whose wavelength is greater than that of visible light; sometimes known as thermal radiation

spectrum: waves, or colours of light, separated out in order according to their wavelengths

Exercise 15.1

IN THIS EXERCISE YOU WILL:

- describe the uses of members of the electromagnetic spectrum
- practise extended writing in the context of the electromagnetic spectrum
- explain how electromagnetic waves have many different uses.

TIP

The electromagnetic spectrum is a term that includes ALL the waves coming from the Sun. It is continuous – there are no gaps/breaks between each member of the spectrum. For example, radio waves are just like long wavelength microwaves. We split the spectrum up according to the energy each member delivers.

Focus

1   The electromagnetic spectrum is the spectrum of all types of electromagnetic radiation, arranged according to their frequencies.

    a   State which type of electromagnetic radiation has the highest frequency. ....

    b   State which type of electromagnetic radiation has the longest wavelength. ....

    c   State which type of electromagnetic radiation has a frequency just greater than that of

        visible light. ....

    d   State which type of electromagnetic radiation has the most damaging effects on the human

        body. ....

Practice

2 Here are a list of types of electromagnetic radiation (on the left) and a list of their uses (on the right). But the lists are not in order.

Draw lines to link each type of electromagnetic radiation with its correct use. There is just one use for each type of radiation.

gamma rays
X-rays
ultraviolet
visible light
infrared
microwaves
radio waves

eyesight
transmitting TV programmes
airport baggage scanners
grilling food
sterilising medical equipment
communicating with spacecraft
forgery detection (banknotes)

Challenge

3 Electromagnetic radiations have many different uses. For each of the following, explain how the type of radiation is used for the purpose mentioned, and what property it has that makes it suitable for this use. You may have to do some research to find the answers.

a X-rays are used in medical diagnosis.

....

....

....

....

....

....

....

b Infrared is used in remote control devices.

....

....

....

....

....

....

c   Microwaves are used to carry mobile phone signals.

....

....

....

....

....

....

....

....

> **TIP**
>
> The wavelengths of electromagnetic waves can be very small and the frequencies very large. A common mistake is to incorrectly convert these numbers into metres or hertz. Take care with your powers of ten!

Figure 15.1: Infrared can be used in remote controls for using the television.

Exercise 15.2

> practise explaining why certain members of the spectrum are used in communications

> describe differences between analogue and digital signals.

Focus

1   a   State what kind of wave is used for Bluetooth communication.

....

    b   State what kind of wave is used for wireless internet.

....

    c   State what kind of wave is used for transmitting data through optic fibres.

....

Practice

2   A learner suggests that X-rays could be used for Bluetooth communication. State what properties of X-rays make this:

    a   a good idea.

....

    b   a bad idea.

....

3   Describe the properties required by a wave used for wireless internet.

....

....

Challenge

4   Compare analogue and digital signal transmission.

In your answer, consider:

- the difference between analogue and digital signals

- the benefits of digital when compared to analogue.

Draw a diagram of an analogue wave and a digital wave as part of your answer.

....

....

....

....

....

....

PEER ASSESSMENT

Create a set of flash cards of the electromagnetic spectrum. You might choose to do this on paper or use a free online program. In your flash cards, you should include:

a   the direction of increasing frequency

b   the direction of decreasing wavelength

c   the order of the colours of visible light within the overall electromagnetic spectrum

d   uses of each member of the spectrum.

Now share your flash cards with others whilst you use theirs. Compare your sets and feed back to the author of the other sets:

What did you like?

How could they improve theirs?

Were there any errors?

Chapter 16

Magnetism

> Permanent magnets and electromagnets

KEY WORDS

magnet: a device which exerts a force on magnetic materials

magnetic material: common magnetic materials are iron, steel, nickel, cobalt

magnetisation: causing a piece of material to be magnetised; a material is magnetised when it produces a magnetic field around itself

soft magnetic material: a material that, once magnetised, can easily be demagnetised, e.g. soft iron

hard magnetic material: a material that, once magnetised, is difficult to demagnetise, e.g. steel

electromagnet: when current is passed through a solenoid, it becomes a magnet; this kind of magnet can be turned on and off and the strength can be controlled by the size of the current flowing through the solenoid

solenoid: a long narrow coil of wire

TIP

Consider each atom of a magnetic material as a little magnet. Before it is magnetised, these 'atomic' magnets are pointing in random directions. Magnetising the material is the process of making these 'atomic' magnets line up, so that they point in the same direction. The more that line up, the stronger the magnetic field around the material. De-magnetising is the reverse of this, and causes the arrangement to be random again. This can be done by shock (hitting it with a hammer), heating it or applying another magnetic field.

Exercise 16.1

IN THIS EXERCISE YOU WILL:

- check your understanding of what a magnet is
- describe how to distinguish between a magnet and a magnetic material
- describe the attractive and repulsive forces between magnets.

Focus

1 What is a magnet?

....

2 Figure 16.1 shows two bar magnets. One pole has been labelled. They are repelling each other.

Figure 16.1: Two bar magnets repelling each other.

    a Label the other three poles in such a way that the magnets will repel each other.

    b Draw force arrows to show the magnetic force on each magnet.

3 In Figure 16.2, the two bar magnets are attracting each other.

Figure 16.2: Two bar magnets attracting each other.

Label their four poles and draw force arrows appropriately to show the magnetic force on each magnet.

Practice

4 Figure 16.3 shows a horseshoe-shaped permanent magnet attracting a steel rod. The attraction shows that magnetic poles are induced in the rod.

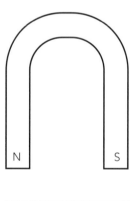

Figure 16.3: A permanent horseshoe magnet attracting a steel rod.

    a State and explain what type of pole (N or S) must be induced in end A of the rod.

       ....

    b State what type of pole (N or S) must be induced in end B. ....

Challenge

5   Describe a method by which you could directly measure the strength of an electromagnet's field, by measuring the force produced by it, and compare the strengths of different electromagnets. You should note the factors that affect the strength of the field and how you would vary them.

....

....

....

....

....

....

....

....

....

Exercise 16.2

IN THIS EXERCISE YOU WILL:

consider why magnets exert forces.

Focus

1   Why do two magnets exert a force on each other?

....

Practice

2   You are given two pieces of metal which look the same. One is iron, the other is steel. Explain how can you tell which is which.

....

....

....

Challenge

3 Research why a compass is not very useful for getting to the North or South poles. Outline your findings.

....

....

....

....

Exercise 16.3

IN THIS EXERCISE YOU WILL:

- check your understanding of the differences between permanent magnets and electromagnets and their uses
- explain how the direction of current flow around the end of the solenoid leads to a N pole and a S pole.

Focus

1 State why an electromagnet is useful.

....

....

Practice

2 Explain whether you would you use soft iron or steel for an electromagnet.

....

....

3 Describe a method by which you could determine the polarity of an electromagnet.

....

....

....

....

Challenge

4   A woman was doing some work on her house. She was using a power drill to make a hole in a steel sheet. A stray piece of metal flew off the drill and hit her in the eye. When she went to hospital, the doctor used a very strong magnet to remove the metal. State whether a permanent magnet or an electromagnet would be most suitable to remove the metal. Explain your answer.

....

5   Describe a method by which you could directly measure the strength of an electromagnet's field, by measuring the force produced by it, and compare the strengths of different electromagnets. You should note the factors that affect the strength of the field and how you would vary them.

....

....

....

....

〉 Magnetic fields

KEY WORDS

magnetic field line: the direction of a magnetic field line at a point in the magnetic field is the direction of the force on a North pole placed at that point

magnetic field: the region of space around a magnet or electric current in which a magnet will feel a force

Exercise 16.4

IN THIS EXERCISE YOU WILL:

- recall that magnetic field lines are used to represent the shape of a magnetic field
- explain how the pattern of magnetic field lines can be used to tell if two magnets are attracting each other, or repelling
- check your understanding magnetic field patterns and your ability to sketch them.

TIP

Magnetic field lines never touch and they never cross.

Focus

1   Complete the four diagrams in Figure 16.4. Draw the magnetic field around the single magnet, around each pair of magnets, and around the electromagnet.

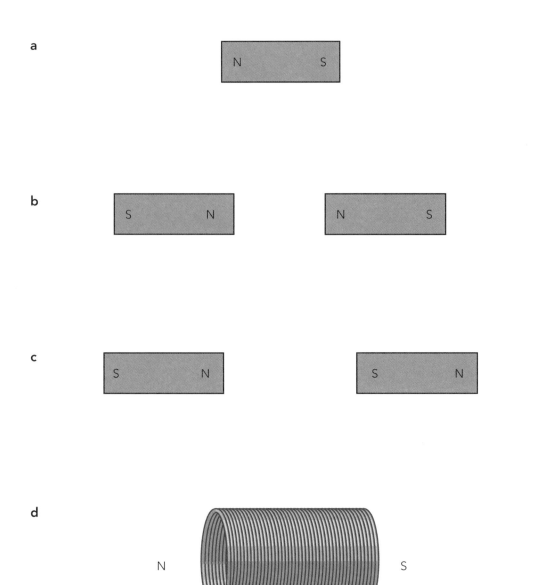

Figure 16.4: Four different magnetic scenarios.

Practice

2 Describe a method that you can use to find the shape of the magnetic field around a bar magnet. Your method should include how you can determine the direction of the field lines.

....

....

....

....

....

....

....

....

Challenge

3 Complete Figure 16.5 by drawing the field pattern between the poles.

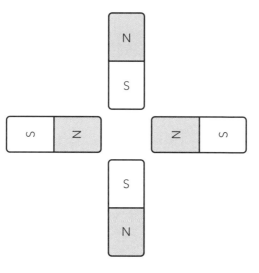

Figure 16.5: Four bar magnets.

4 Explain why two North poles or two South poles repel.

....

....

....

....

5 Sketch the magnetic field around a strong permanent bar magnet and a weak permanent magnet, so that it is clear which is which, without labels.

TIP

Always mark the direction of the field lines on the diagram when you draw it.

PEER ASSESSMENT

Make a set of flash cards to cover the key facts on magnetism and electromagnetism. You might choose to do this on paper or use a free online programme.

Now share your flash cards with others whilst you use theirs. Compare your sets and feed back to the author of the other set:

- What did you like?
- How could they improve theirs?
- Were there any errors?

> Chapter 17
Static electricity
> ## Charging and discharging

Exercise 17.1

IN THIS EXERCISE YOU WILL:

- recall key facts about the attractive and repulsive forces between electric charges
- check your understanding of electrostatic charging
- describe how an object gains an electrostatic charge by thinking about electrons and protons.

TIP

NEVER talk about positive charge moving with static electricity. It is ALWAYS (negative) electrons.

Focus

1 a What name is given to a material that allows electric charge to flow through it?

   ....

  b Give an example of a material that does allow charge to flow through it.

   ....

2 A learner rubs a plastic rod with a wool cloth. The rod gains a negative electrostatic charge. Before the experiment, the rod had no electrostatic charge.

   State the one word that means 'having no electrostatic charge'. ....

Practice

3 **a** State what type of particles have been transferred to the rod in Question 2. Explain how you know.

....

....

b The cloth is left with a positive charge. State which type of particle it has more of:

protons or electrons. ....

4 A learner rubs a plastic rod with a wool cloth. The rod and cloth both become electrostatically charged.

a State the force that causes the two materials to become charged. ....

b The cloth has a positive electrostatic charge. State what type of charge the rod has.

....

c The cloth and rod are brought close to one another. State whether they will they attract or

repel each other. ....

d Explain why this happens.

....

....

....

....

5 Figure 17.1 shows one way in which the learner could observe the forces exerted by the electrostatically charged cloth and rod on each other.

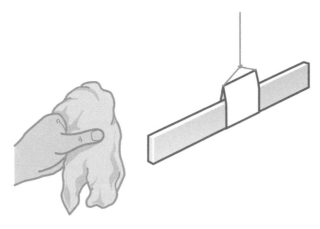

Figure 17.1: A diagram showing how the electrostatic forces between two charged objects might be observed.

Write a brief description of this experiment. Explain how it is done and describe what you would expect to observe.

....

....

....

....

....

....

....

....

Challenge

6   Explain why conductors allow electrostatic charge to flow through them, but other materials do not allow charge to flow through them.

....

....

....

....

....

....

> Explaining static electricity

Exercise 17.2

IN THIS EXERCISE YOU WILL:

practise explaining everyday static electricity phenomena.

Focus

1   It is easy to generate static electricity by rubbing two materials together. The materials must both be electrical insulators, and they must not be the same material.

Find some different plastic items such as pens, rulers and combs. Find some pieces of cloth made from cotton, polyester, wool and so on.

Rub one plastic item on one of the cloths. Test whether your item has become electrostatically charged by seeing if it will pick up scraps of paper. Use scraps of thin paper less than 5 mm in size.

Try different combinations of plastic items and cloths. Keep a record of your results in a table.

Describe and explain your findings briefly. In your answer:

- state whether one combination of materials is better than another at generating static electricity

- describe how you made this a fair test.

....

....

....

....

....

....

....

....

....

....

....

....

Practice

2   Use a comb on clean, dry hair that does not have any hair product in it (such as hair gel, conditioner, etc.). Pass the comb through your hair many times.

Now bring the comb very close to (but NOT touching) a slow steady stream of water from a tap.

a Describe what you see happening.

....

....

....

....

b Explain your observations.

....

....

....

....

PEER ASSESSMENT

Discuss your explanation with your class.

Challenge

3 Explain why we sometimes get a shock when we walk across a carpet and touch a door handle.

....

....

....

....

....

> Electric fields and electric charge

KEY WORD

electric field: a region where charged objects experience force; the direction of the field at a point in the field is the direction of force on positive charge

Exercise 17.3

IN THIS EXERCISE YOU WILL:

> practise drawing electric field patterns.

TIP

With field patterns, how closely packed the field lines are shows us how strong the field is. Field lines ALWAYS go from positive to negative.

Focus

1   State the direction of an electric field at a point.

    ....

Practice

2   Draw the field patterns described:

    a   around an isolated positive charge.

b   around a negatively charged sphere.

c   between two parallel plates that have a potential difference between them.

Challenge

3   Draw the field pattern between the charges shown in Figure 17.2.

Figure 17.2: A diagram showing two point charges close to each other.

> Chapter 18
Electrical quantities
› Current in electric circuits

KEY WORDS

p.d. (potential difference): another name for the voltage between two points

electromotive force (e.m.f): the electrical work done in moving +1 C around a complete circuit

amp, ampere (A): the SI unit of electric current

coulomb (C): the SI unit of electric charge; $1\,C = 1\,A\,s$ ('1 amp-second')

ohm (Ω): the SI unit of electrical resistance; $1\,\Omega = 1\,V/A$ ('1 volt per amp')

volt (V): the SI unit of voltage (p.d. or e.m.f.); $1\,V = 1\,J/C$ ('1 joule per coulomb')

current: a flow of electric charge

current: the charge passing a point in a circuit per unit time

conductor: a substance that allows an electric current to pass through it

insulator: a substance that does not conduct electricity

voltage: the 'push' of a battery or power supply in a circuit

cell: a device that provides a potential difference in a circuit

battery: two or more electrical cells connected together in series; the word may also be used to mean a single cell

battery capacity: a measure of the stored energy. Measured in Ah ('amp-hours')

KEY EQUATIONS

$I = \dfrac{Q}{t}$, where I = current in amps, Q = charge in coulombs and t = time in seconds

$E = \dfrac{W}{Q}$

potential difference (in volts) = $\dfrac{\text{work done}}{\text{charge}}$

e.m.f. (in volts) = $\dfrac{\text{work done}}{\text{charge}}$

> **TIP**
>
> Note the subtle difference between the definition of potential difference (p.d.) and the definition of electromotive force (e.m.f.). Potential difference is the work done in moving +1 coulomb (C) between two points in a circuit, whereas e.m.f. is the work done in moving +1 C around the whole circuit.

Exercise 18.1

IN THIS EXERCISE YOU WILL:

practise your understanding of basic ideas about electric circuits.

Focus

1   **a**   For an electric current to flow, it must have something to flow through. Complete the table by putting a tick (✓) in the correct column to indicate whether the material listed is a conductor or an insulator.

Material	Conductor?	Insulator?
steel		
plastic		
glass		
copper		
silver		
wood		

b   Describe an experiment, using an ammeter, which would allow you to prove that your answers above are correct. State what you would expect to see.

....

....

....

....

....

....

....

....

Practice

2   Figure 18.1 shows a simple circuit.

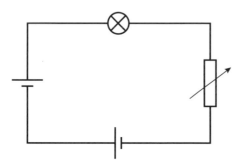

Figure 18.1: A simple circuit.

    a   Draw a labelled arrow to show the direction of the current in the circuit.

    b   Draw a labelled arrow to show the direction of flow of free electrons in the circuit.

3   The circuit in Figure 18.2 has two meters. Their symbols are incomplete.

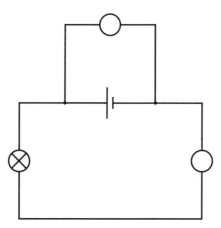

Figure 18.2: A simple circuit with two unknown meters.

    a   Complete the symbol for the meter that measures the current. Label it with its name.

    b   Complete the symbol for the meter that measures the voltage of the cell. Label it with its name.

    c   State the name given to two or more cells connected together in a circuit. ....

4   Describe how connecting cells in parallel affects the p.d. across the arrangement.

....

Challenge

5   In the circuit in Question **2**, the p.d. across the circuit is doubled. At the same time, two more identical lamps are added in series. Describe what effect that will have on the current. Show your working.

....

....

....

6   Two 1.5 V cells are connected in parallel across a fixed resistor. Describe what effect this has on the current through the resistor.

....

Exercise 18.2

IN THIS EXERCISE YOU WILL:

- show that an electric current is a flow of electric charge (the same charge that helps us to explain static electricity)

> explain the relationship between charge, current and time

> describe the difference between electron flow and conventional current flow in a metal.

Focus

1   When there is a current in a circuit, electrons move through the metal wires.

Figure 18.3 shows a simple circuit in which a cell makes a current flow around the circuit.

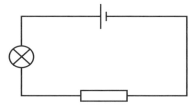

Figure 18.3: A simple circuit with a cell.

Draw an arrow on the circuit to show the direction of electron flow and label it 'electron flow'.

Practice

2 **a** The equation $Q = It$ relates current, charge and time. Complete the table to show the meaning of the symbols in this equation and give their units (name and symbol).

Symbol for quantity	Quantity	Unit (name and symbol)
Q		
I		
t		

b Write an equation linking the following units: coulomb, ampere and second.

....

3 **a** A current of 2.4 A flows in a circuit. State how much charge flows past a point in one

second. ....

b Calculate the charge that flows in 30 s. ....

4 An electric motor is supplied with current by a power supply. A charge of 720 C passes through the motor each minute. Calculate the current that is flowing.

....

5 **a** A battery supplies a current of 1.25 A to a circuit. Calculate how long it will take for 75 C of charge to flow round the circuit.

....

b If this battery has a capacity of 10 Ah, calculate how long can it supply this current.

....

Challenge

6 During a journey in a car, a p.d. of 500 V builds up, due to the static charge on the car caused by friction. A charge of 500 mC is stored on the car. When the driver gets out and touches the car, this charge passes through the driver in 0.1 seconds. By calculating the current, explain why this 500 V p.d. is not lethal (will cause death), but mains potential difference is.

....

....

....

⟩ Electrical resistance

KEY WORDS

resistance: the ratio of the p.d. across a component to the current flowing through it

amp, ampere (A): the SI unit of electric current

ohm (Ω): the SI unit of electrical resistance; $1\,\Omega = 1\,V/A$ ('1 volt per amp')

volt (V): the SI unit of voltage (p.d. or e.m.f.); $1\,V = 1\,J/C$ ('1 joule per coulomb')

resistor: a component in an electric circuit which limits or controls the current flowing

KEY EQUATION

$$resistance = \frac{potential\ difference}{current}$$

$$R = \frac{V}{I}$$

Exercise 18.3

IN THIS EXERCISE YOU WILL:

- show how the resistance of a component tells us how easy (or difficult) it is to make current flow through that component

- practise calculations using the equation $R = \dfrac{V}{I}$.

Focus

1   We say that an ohm (Ω) is a volt (V) per ampere (A). So, if a resistor has a resistance of $10\,\Omega$, it takes 10 V to make a current of 1 A flow through it.

    a   Calculate the voltage needed to make a current of 2 A flow through the same $10\,\Omega$ resistor.

        ....

    b   Calculate the voltage needed to make a current of 1 A flow through a $20\,\Omega$ resistor.

        ....

Practice

2 The current in a circuit changes as the resistance in the circuit changes. Complete the table by indicating whether the change indicated will cause the current to increase or to decrease.

Change	Current – increase or decrease?
more resistance in the circuit	
less resistance in the circuit	
increase the voltage	
use thinner wires	
use longer wires	

Challenge

3 Use the equation $R = \dfrac{V}{I}$ to calculate the resistance of a lamp if a p.d. of 36 V makes a current

of 4.5 A flow through it.

....

4 A learner measured the resistance of a resistor. To do this, she set up a circuit in which the resistor was connected to a variable power supply, a voltmeter and an ammeter.

a In the space, draw a circuit diagram to represent these components connected together correctly so that the learner could measure the current in the resistor and the p.d. across it.

b The table shows the learner's results. Complete the third column. The first one has been done for you.

P.d. V(V)	Current I(A)	Resistance R(Ω)
2.0	0.37	5.4
4.1	0.75	
5.9	1.20	
7.9	1.60	

c Calculate an average value for the resistance R of the resistor.

....

Exercise 18.4

IN THIS EXERCISE YOU WILL:

> discuss how changing the length or diameter of a wire alters its resistance.

Focus

1 How does doubling the length of a wire change its resistance?

....

Practice

2 How does doubling the diameter of a wire affect its resistance?

....

Challenge

3 A wire has a resistance of $5\,\Omega$. Calculate the resistance of a wire of the same material that is three times as long and twice as thick.

....

> More about electrical resistance

Exercise 18.5

IN THIS EXERCISE YOU WILL:

- recall that the resistance of a component may change if the current through it is changed

> explain that a current–voltage characteristic graph can show how the resistance of a component may change if the current through it is changed

> practise using graphs of current against potential difference to answer questions about some common circuit components.

Focus

1 A learner set up the circuit in Figure 18.4 to find out how the current in a filament lamp changed when the potential difference (p.d.) across it was changed.

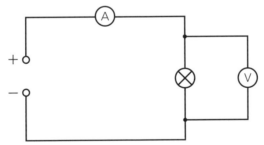

Figure 18.4: A circuit used to find how the current varies through a filament lamp when the p.d. across it is varied.

a On the circuit diagram, write the name of each component shown.

b The ammeter is connected in series with the lamp. State how the voltmeter is connected.

....

....

2   The learner changed the p.d. across the lamp and recorded the values of p.d. *V* and current *I* each time. The table shows his results.

P.d. V(V)	Current I(A)	Resistance $R(\Omega)$
0.0	0.0	—
2.0	0.10	
4.0	0.18	
6.0	0.25	
8.0	0.31	
10.0	0.36	
12.0	0.40	

Complete the last column of the table by calculating the value of the lamp's resistance for each value of the p.d.

Practice

3   Describe how the lamp's resistance in Question **2** changed as the p.d. was increased.

....

....

4   a   On the grid provided, draw a graph to show how the current increased as the p.d. across the lamp in Question **2** increased. This is the current–voltage characteristic for the lamp.

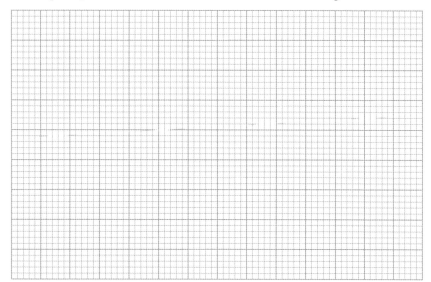

b From your graph, deduce the current in the lamp when there is a p.d. of 5.0 V across it.

....

c From your graph, deduce the p.d. needed to make a current of 0.30 A flow in the lamp.

....

5 Many resistors are described as 'ohmic'. This means that their resistance does not change as the p.d. across them changes. On the small grid, sketch the shape of the current–voltage characteristic graph for such a resistor.

Challenge

6 Explain the changing shape of the graph in Question **5**.

....

....

....

....

....

〉 Electricity and energy

KEY WORDS

power: the rate at which work is done or energy is transferred

watt (W): the SI unit of power; 1 W = 1 J/s

direct current (d.c.): electric current that flows in the same direction all the time

alternating current (a.c.): electric current that flows first one way, then the other, in a circuit

---

KEY EQUATIONS

power = current × p.d.

$P = I \times V$

---

energy transformed = current × p.d. × time

$E = I \times V \times t$

---

energy (kWh) = power of appliance (kW) × time used (hours)

cost of using an electrical appliance = power of appliance (kW) × time used (hours) × cost per unit

---

Exercise 18.6

IN THIS EXERCISE YOU WILL:

- recall that power is the rate at which energy is transferred
- practise your understanding of power in electrical circuits.

TIP

If we were to compare a 40 watt (W) lamp and a 100 W lamp, both of which are at normal brightness with 230 V across them, which would have the higher resistance? Power is given by $P = V \times I$, but in both cases the potential difference is the same, so it is a rise in the current that causes the increase in power (from 40 W to 100 W). To have a larger current with the same potential difference requires a lower resistance (from $V = I \times R$, so $I = \frac{V}{R}$).

Therefore, a higher-powered lamp has a lower resistance.

Focus

1 a Write down an equation linking power, energy transformed and time.

....

   b Write down an equation linking power, current and p.d.

....

Practice

TIP
Electricity calculations very often involve conversions between units, such as kW to W, minutes to seconds etc. Watch out for these.

2 An electric motor is connected to a 12 V direct current (d.c.) supply. A current of 0.25 A flows through the motor.

Calculate the power of the motor.

....

....

3 An electrical appliance has a label that indicates its power. The label includes the following data:

110 V   500 W   50 Hz

   a State the power rating of the appliance. ....

   b State how much energy it transfers each second. ....

   c State how you can tell that the appliance works with alternating current (a.c).

....

   d Calculate the current that will flow when the appliance is in normal use.

....

....

Challenge

4 A lamp has a resistance of 600 Ω.

   a Calculate the current that flows through the lamp when it is connected to a 240 V mains supply.

....

....

b   Calculate the power of the lamp.

....

....

5   Complete the table below. The cost per kWh is 20 pence.

Potential difference / V	Current / A	Power / W	Time used for / mins	Cost of use for this time / pence
200		600		3.6
	2.72	600	90	
120	4			16
200 000		300 000	10	1000
220		100	240	

PEER ASSESSMENT

Draw a mind map of the chapter, then compare your mind map to those of others. Give and receive feedback on the mind maps.

> Chapter 19

Electrical circuits

> Circuit components

KEY WORDS

variable resistor: a resistor whose resistance can be changed, for example by turning a knob

light-dependent resistor (LDR): a device whose resistance decreases when light shines on it

thermistor: a resistor whose resistance changes a lot over a small temperature range

potential divider: a part of a circuit used to provide a variable potential difference

potential divider: two resistors connected in series to provide a variable potential difference

diode: an electrical component that allows electric current to flow in one direction only

light-emitting diode (LED): a type of diode that emits light when a current flows through it

---

KEY EQUATION

Total potential difference for two resistors used as a potential divider:
resistance of resistor 1 / resistance of resistor 2 = p.d. of resistor 1 / p.d. of resistor 2

$$\frac{R_1}{R_2} = \frac{V_1}{V_2}$$

TIP

The whole of electricity depends on two things:

The principle of conservation of energy: the total energy gained (per coulomb) across the power supply = total energy lost (per coulomb) in getting back to the power supply again, no matter what path the current takes.

The conservation of charge: if a current flows into a point in the circuit, ALL of it must flow back out again.

Together these explain series and parallel circuits.

Exercise 19.1

Focus

1   Complete the following table by drawing the symbol for each component.

lamp	resistor	variable resistor
LDR	thermistor	fuse
switch	cell	motor

Practice

2   Complete the table by identifying each component described in the first column. The component names are all in the table in the previous question.

Description	Component
gives out heat and light	
resistance changes as the temperature changes	

Description	Component
provides the 'push' to make a current flow	
'blows' when the current is too high	
makes and breaks a circuit	
has less resistance on a sunny day	
adjusted to change the resistance in a circuit	

Challenge

3   Using the symbol in Figure 19.1 for a variable potential divider, draw a circuit that allows the p.d. across a lamp to be varied from 0 V to 12 V.

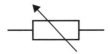

Figure 19.1: Symbol for a variable potential divider.

4   Figure 19.2 shows the circuit for a potential divider. The p.d. across R_1 is 8 V. Calculate the ratio $R_1:R_2$

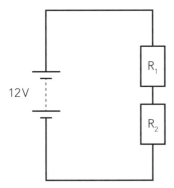

Figure 19.2: A potential divider circuit consisting of two resistors.

....

....

Exercise 19.2

IN THIS EXERCISE YOU WILL:

> practise applying your knowledge and understanding of what a diode does and how it might be used.

Focus

1   Draw a diode in a circuit with a cell and a lamp so that current will flow.

Practice

2   Why might a diode be a good idea in a circuit?

....

....

Challenge

3   In the rather complicated-looking circuit in Figure 19.3, there are several lamps, several light-dependent resistors (LDRs), and several light-emitting diodes (LEDs).

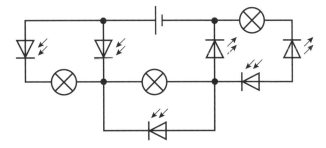

Figure 19.3: A circuit consisting of several filament lamps and LEDs with a cell.

a   For each LED, decide whether or not it will light up. Mark each LED that lights up with a tick (✓)

b   For each lamp, decide whether or not it will light up. Mark each lamp that lights up with a tick (✓)

〉 Combinations of resistors

Exercise 19.3

IN THIS EXERCISE YOU WILL:

practise applying your knowledge and understanding of how current flows in a circuit with more than one resistor.

Focus

1 Calculate the combined resistance of four $120\,\Omega$ resistors connected in series.

   ....

2 Look at the circuit shown in Figure 19.4.

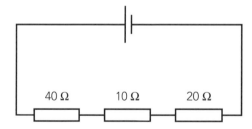

Figure 19.4: A circuit consisting of three resistors of specified values and a cell.

State whether the three resistors are connected in series or in parallel. ....

Practice

3   **a**   Calculate the combined resistance of the three resistors in Question **2**.

....

   b   Describe the nature of the current in this circuit.

....

....

4   Look at the circuit shown in Figure 19.5.

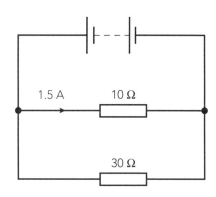

Figure 19.5: A circuit consisting of a battery and two resistors of specified values.

   a   State whether the two resistors are connected in series or in parallel. ....

   b   One of the following statements is true. Tick (✓) the correct one.

   A   The combined resistance of the two resistors must be less than $10\,\Omega$.   ☐

   B   The combined resistance of the two resistors must be more than $40\,\Omega$.   ☐

Challenge

5   The diagram shows that the current in the $30\,\Omega$ resistor is 1.5 A. Calculate the current in the $30\,\Omega$ resistor in Question **4**.

....

Exercise 19.4

IN THIS EXERCISE YOU WILL:

practise applying your knowledge and understanding of series and in parallel arrangements of cells and resistors.

Focus

1 Three batteries, with e.m.f.s E_1, E_2 and E_3, are connected in series. State the total e.m.f. of this arrangement.

....

2 Explain why we sometimes connect cells in parallel.

....

3 Calculate the combined resistance of four $120\,\Omega$ resistors connected in parallel.

....

> ### TIP
>
> You might wonder why we connect resistors in parallel like this. Why not just pick a single resistor with the correct value? The answer is that the resistance of a resistor isn't exactly what it says – there is a variation, of perhaps ± 10%, which is called the *tolerance*. Therefore, to make sure you get as close to the stated value as you can, you use resistors of other values in parallel to make the correct overall resistance, and then these ± 10% variations usually cancel out.

Practice

4 Figure 19.6 shows three resistors connected to a battery.

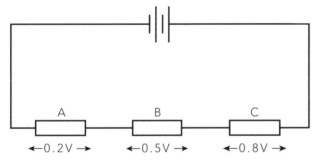

Figure 19.6: A circuit consisting of a battery and three resistors, A, B and C.

a By comparing the p.d.s across the resistors, determine which resistor has the greatest resistance. ....

b A current of 0.15 A flows through resistor A. Calculate the resistance of resistor C.

....

c Calculate the p.d. of the battery.

....

....

5   In Figure 19.7, resistors A and B are connected in parallel to a 12 V battery. The current flowing from the battery and the current through resistor A are marked on the circuit diagram.

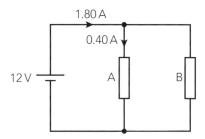

Figure 19.7: A circuit consisting of a battery and two resistors in parallel.

a   Calculate the resistance of resistor A.

....

b   Explain the benefit of wiring devices in parallel.

....

c   Calculate the current through resistor B. Explain your answer.

....

....

d   Calculate the resistance of resistor B.

....

6   A solar cell is required to produce the same current throughout its operation. The p.d. across it varies with light level. State what must change in the circuit, to ensure the current remains constant as the p.d. rises.

....

Challenge

7   Calculate the combined (effective) resistance of A and B in Question **5**.

....

....

8   Two cells of e.m.f. E_1 and E_2 are connected in series across a resistor, resistance $R\,\Omega$. The current flowing is 4 A. One of the cells is now reversed. The current flowing is 2 A. Calculate the value of $\dfrac{E_1}{E_2}$.

....

....

....

....

....

....

> Electronic circuits

KEY EQUATION

total potential difference for two resistors used as a potential divider = resistance of resistor 1 / resistance of resistor 2 = p.d. of resistor 1 / p.d. or resistor 2

$$\frac{R_1}{R_2} = \frac{V_1}{V_2}$$

Exercise 19.5

IN THIS EXERCISE YOU WILL:

practise applying your knowledge and understanding of light dependent resistors and how they can be used.

Figure 19.8 shows a circuit that can act as a light sensor.

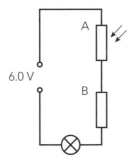

Figure 19.8: A circuit acting as a light sensor.

Focus

1 a Label the following components in the circuit in Figure 19.8:

     LDR   lamp

  b State what happens to the resistance of the LDR when light falls on it.

     ....

Practice

2 State what effect this will have on the p.d. across resistor **B**.

     ....

Challenge

3 In Figure 19.9, we have added an additional component to the circuit from Question **1** and there is another circuit, with a lamp in it, next to the first circuit.

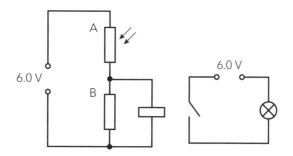

Figure 19.9: A circuit acting as a light sensor to control another circuit containing a filament lamp and battery.

  a State the name of this new component.

     ....

  b Explain briefly why this will cause the lamp to light up.

     ....

     ....

     ....

     ....

  c State **one** possible use for this circuit.

     ....

     ....

d Describe how the circuit could be adapted so that the lamp lights up when the temperature drops.

....

....

e State which two components form a potential divider. ....

> Electrical safety

KEY WORDS

fuse: a device used to prevent excessive currents flowing in a circuit

trip switch: a safety device that automatically switches off a circuit when the current becomes too high

Exercise 19.6

IN THIS EXERCISE YOU WILL:

describe how we use mains electricity safely.

Focus

1 Many countries do not allow light switches or power sockets to be fitted in bathrooms.

Explain why this is the case.

....

2 a A fuse relies on the earth wire to work.

State why some devices must have an earth wire, whilst others do not require one.

....

b State where the earth wire is connected to, apart from the device.

....

Practice

3   Describe what safety issue Figure 19.10 shows.

Figure 19.10: A domestic wall socket in use.

....

....

4   Sometimes, when a fuse breaks, people replace it with a piece of metal foil.

a   Explain the operation of a fuse.

....

....

b   Explain why the fuse is a safety device.

....

....

c   State and what the worst-case scenario for the house might be if the fuse is replaced with metal foil. Explain your answer.

....

....

....

....

Challenge

5   Explain the operation of a trip switch.

....

....

6 State the sequence of events that leads to the fuse melting.

....

....

....

....

....

7 Someone is operating an electric hedge cutter whilst standing on wet grass. The cable is cut by accident. Explain why it is unlikely that a fuse will save the life of the operator.

....

....

8 Two 12 V, 40 W lamps are connected in series and are shining with normal brightness. State what will be seen if one of the lamps is removed and replaced with a 12 V, 100 W lamp. Explain your answer. Show your working.

....

....

....

....

....

9 Draw a circuit that will only allow current to flow clockwise, allowing a user to adjust the light level at which a lamp will turn on.

PEER ASSESSMENT

After you have completed each of Questions **8** and **9**, get feedback on the strengths and development areas in your answers from others in your class and do the same for them.

Chapter 20

Electromagnetic forces

> The magnetic effect of a current

Exercise 20.1

IN THIS EXERCISE YOU WILL:

- practise applying your understanding of the magnetic effect of an electric current
- explain how we make use of this effect in a number of devices.

Focus

1   The direction of the magnetic field lines around a current is given by the 'right-hand grip rule'. You imagine gripping the wire with your right hand.

Complete the following sentences:

a   The direction of your thumb tells you the direction of ....

b   The direction in which your fingers curl round the wire tells you the direction of

....

2   A relay is an electromagnetically operated switch. Figure 20.1 shows a circuit that makes use of a relay.

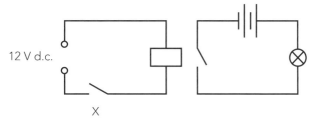

Figure 20.1: A circuit diagram showing a relay in use.

a Copy the circuit symbol for the relay into the space below. Label the parts of it that represent the coil and the switch.

b Why are relays used? State **one** use of a relay.

....

Practice

3 State and explain what happens when switch X in the circuit shown in Question **2** is closed.

....

....

....

....

4 Describe an experiment to establish the shape of the magnetic field around a long straight wire.

....

....

....

....

....

....

....

....

....

Challenge

5 **a** Sketch the magnetic field around a solenoid, carrying a current. Label the direction of the current flow and the direction of the field lines.

b Describe an experiment to verify this experimentally.

....

....

....

....

....

....

....

....

6 A 10 m length of wire has a current of 5 A flowing through it. It is then coiled tightly into a solenoid. State how the magnetic field strength would compare between the two situations, at equal distances from each.

....

....

7 **a** Describe the effect on the magnetic field around a solenoid of increasing the current flowing through the solenoid.

....

....

b State how the polarity of the solenoid could be reversed.

....

⟩ How electric motors are constructed

KEY WORDS

electromagnet: a coil of wire that becomes a magnet when a current flows in it

commutator: a device used to allow current to flow to and from the coil of a d.c. motor or generator

Exercise 20.2

IN THIS EXERCISE YOU WILL:

- explain how an electric motor is constructed.

Focus

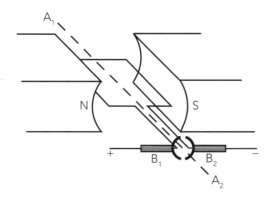

Figure 20.2: An electric motor.

1 **a** An electric motor (Figure 20.2) can be made using a coil of wire that rotates in a magnetic field.

  Name the part of the motor that acts as an electromagnet. ....

  b Electric current enters and leaves the coil via two brushes. Name the part of the motor

  against which the brushes press, to transfer the current to the coil. ....

Practice

2 State how the turning effect of a d.c. motor can be increased.

  ....

  ....

....

....

Challenge

3 Describe the effect on the motor when the directions of both the magnetic field and the current were reversed whilst simultaneously increasing the current.

....

....

....

4 **a** State what would be observed if alternating current was passed through the coil of a d.c. motor.

....

b A learner built a motor to run on a d.c. supply. The learner forgot to include a commutator. State what would be observed when the motor is switched on.

....

5 **a** Figure 20.3 shows a cross-section through a loudspeaker. Label parts 1–3 with their names.

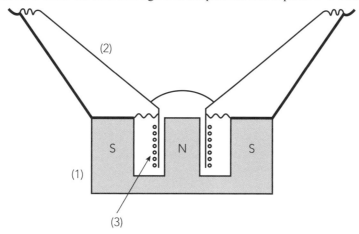

Figure 20.3: Cross-section through a loudspeaker.

b Add field lines to the diagram.

c   Explain how the loudspeaker works. In your answer, consider an instant when the current is flowing out of the page on the left hand side of the coil and into the page on the right hand side of the coil.

....

....

....

....

....

....

....

....

....

d   Compare the loudspeaker and the d.c. motor – consider similarities and differences.

....

....

....

....

....

....

....

....

e   Using your knowledge of forces from Chapters 3 and 12 of the Workbook as well as your knowledge from this section, state and explain the factors to be considered in designing a loudspeaker.

....

....

....

....

....

〉 Force on a current-carrying conductor

Exercise 20.3

Focus

1   State how the direction of the force on a current-carrying conductor could be reversed.

   ....

   ....

   ....

2   Figure 20.4 shows an electron beam tube. The electron gun on the left produces a beam of electrons travelling towards the right.

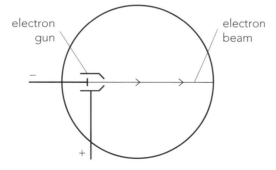

Figure 20.4: An electron beam tube. The electron gun on the left produces a beam of electrons that travel towards the right.

a The electron beam can be thought of as an electric current, since electrons are charged particles.

State the direction of the conventional current in the diagram.

....

b A magnetic field can be used to deflect the electron beam. The field produces a force on the moving electrons. Fleming's left-hand rule gives the direction of the force.

Label the thumb and first two fingers of the left hand in Figure 20.5 to show what each represents.

Figure 20.5: Fleming's left-hand rule.

TIP

The reason that moving electrons experience a force in a magnetic field and stationary ones don't is because magnetic fields are *caused* by moving charge. So when they are moving, the electrons have a magnetic field around them that interacts with the magnetic field they have been placed in.

Practice

3 The apparatus shown in Figure 20.6 is used to demonstrate the force on a current-carrying conductor in a magnetic field.

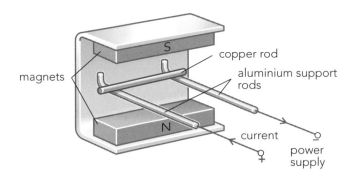

Figure 20.6: Equipment used to demonstrate the force on a conductor carrying a current at right angles to a magnetic field.

a   Draw a line on the diagram to show the direction of the magnetic field.

b   In this arrangement, the force on the copper rod will make it roll towards the power supply. Describe the effect of reversing the direction of the current.

....

....

....

....

c   State **two** ways in which the force on the copper rod could be increased.

....

....

....

....

4   In Figure 20.7, the electron beam has been deflected upwards by a magnetic field.

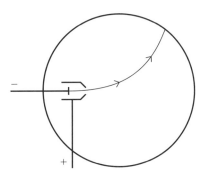

Figure 20.7: A beam of electrons being deflected upwards by a magnetic field.

a   State whether the direction of the magnetic field is into or out of the paper.

....

b   If the magnetic field is reversed so that it is in the opposite direction, the force on the electrons will be in the opposite direction.

Draw a diagram to show the path of the electrons in the tube.

Challenge

5 You want to deflect the beam of electrons horizontally towards you. State which direction you should apply the magnetic field.

....

6 Explain why a magnetic field can deflect a beam of protons but not a beam of neutrons.

....

....

7 You want to deflect a beam of protons by the same amount as a beam of electrons. State the change you would have to make to your experiment. Explain your answer.

....

....

....

....

....

8 Explain why this effect (charged particles moving in a magnetic field) explains the Northern and Southern lights.

....

....

....

PEER ASSESSMENT

Write a set of flash cards or draw a mind map to summarise this chapter.

Swap your work with others in your class and offer feedback to each other.

What was the thing you liked best about the other person's work? Was there anything that you felt needed further development?

Chapter 21

Electromagnetic induction

> Generating electricity

KEY WORDS

electromagnetic induction: the process by which a potential difference is induced across a conductor when the magnetic field around it changes

a.c. generator: a device, such as a dynamo, used to generate alternating current (a.c.)

slip rings: a device used to allow current to flow to and from the coil of an a.c. motor or generator

Fleming's right-hand rule: a rule that gives the relationship between the directions of force, field and current when a current is induced by moving a conductor relative to a magnetic field

Exercise 21.1

IN THIS EXERCISE YOU WILL:

check your understanding of electromagnetic induction.

TIP

If you compare the left- and right-hand rules, you'll see that the only difference is that the induced current flows in the opposite direction (Fleming's right-hand rule) to the current (left-hand rule). If the induced current flowed in the same direction, it would produce a force which would tend to make the conductor accelerate in the same direction as the motion causing it, so it would get faster. This would mean that the induced current would be bigger and so the process repeats. That's a violation of the principle of conservation of energy.

Focus

1   Complete the table by indicating whether a current will be induced (made to flow). In each case, assume that the wire is part of a complete circuit. Write 'Yes' or 'No' in the second column.

Case	Is a current induced?
A wire is moved through the field of a magnet.	
A magnet is held close to a wire.	
A magnet is moved into a coil of wire.	
A magnet is moved out of a coil of wire.	
A magnet rests in a coil of wire.	

Practice

2 Describe how the induced e.m.f. across a coil of wire could be increased.

....

....

....

3 The direction of rotation is reversed. State how this affects the induced e.m.f.

....

Challenge

4 State the one factor that links all of your answers to Question **2**. Explain your answer.

....

....

Exercise 21.2

IN THIS EXERCISE YOU WILL:

> describe how an a.c. generator works

> show how the change in e.m.f. produced over time is related to the position of an a.c. generator coil.

TIP

You'll see three terms used to describe what seems to be the same thing: 'voltage', 'potential difference' (or p.d.) and 'electromotive force' (or e.m.f.). This can be confusing. Potential difference is the work done in moving +1 C between two points in a circuit; e.m.f. is the work done in moving +1 C around the whole circuit. Voltage is really a statement of the value of the potential difference or e.m.f.

Focus

1   Alternating current is generated using an a.c. generator. This is similar to an electric motor, working in reverse. Write the missing word.

An a.c. generator does not have a commutator. Instead, current enters and leaves the spinning

coil through brushes that press on the ....

Practice

2   Figure 21.1 shows how an alternating current varies with time. On the diagram, mark one cycle of the alternating current.

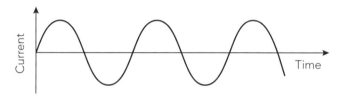

Figure 21.1: The variation of alternating current with time.

Challenge

3   In Figure 21.2, which is a larger version of Figure 21.1, draw the position of the coil when the current is:

a   a maximum positive value

b   zero

c   a maximum negative value.

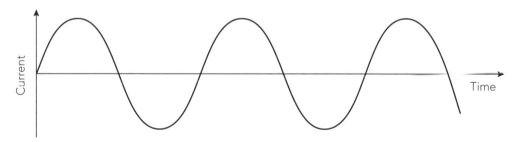

Figure 21.2: The variation of alternating current with time.

> **TIP**
>
> Consider that the North pole of the magnetic field is on the left of the page. The coil begins with the side labelled A next to the North pole and the side labelled B next to the South pole. The coil then turns clockwise.

> Power lines and transformers

KEY WORDS

transformer: a device used to change the voltage of an a.c. electricity supply

power lines: cables used to carry electricity from power stations to consumers

KEY EQUATIONS

$$\frac{\text{voltage across primary coil}}{\text{voltage across secondary coil}} = \frac{\text{number of turns on primary coil}}{\text{number of turns on secondary coil}}$$

$$\frac{V_p}{V_s} = \frac{N_p}{N_s}$$

power into primary coil = power out of secondary coil

$$> \quad I_p \times V_p = I_s \times V_s$$

Power = current² × resistance

$$> \quad P = I^2 R$$

Exercise 21.3

IN THIS EXERCISE YOU WILL:

- check your understanding of how transformers use electromagnetic induction to change the potential difference and thereby the current of an alternating supply
- practise calculating the number of turns on a secondary coil and the power generated by a transformer.

Focus

1   Figure 21.3 shows a step-up transformer. State which coil has more turns in such a transformer.

....

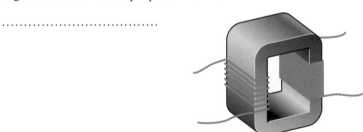

Figure 21.3: A step-up transformer.

2   On figure 21.3, label the primary coil, the secondary coil and the iron core.

Practice

3 In the circuit diagram in Figure 21.4, a transformer is being used to change the mains voltage to a lower value so that it will light a 12 V lamp.

120 V
a.c. mains

lamp

Figure 21.4: A mains transformer used to power a 12 V lamp.

a State whether this is a step-up or step-down transformer. ....

b The primary coil has 1000 turns. Calculate how many turns the secondary coil has.

....

....

....

4 At a small power station, the generator produces alternating current at a voltage of 10 kV. This must be reduced to 415 V for use in a factory.

a The transformer used for this purpose has a primary coil of 2000 turns. Calculate how many turns the secondary coil has.

....

....

....

b In normal operation, the current flowing from the generator is 4.5 A. Calculate the power that is being generated.

....

....

....

c Calculate the current flowing in the power lines in the factory. Assume that all of the electrical power generated is transmitted to the factory.

....

....

....

Challenge

5 An overhead power line has a resistance of 2.5 Ω. By considering the power losses, find the increase in efficiency when transmitting 100 MW of electrical energy along this cable at:

a 20 000 V

....

....

....

b 400 000 V.

....

....

....

> How transformers work

Exercise 21.4

IN THIS EXERCISE YOU WILL:

check your understanding of how transformers work.

Focus

1 State the name of the effect that transformers need to work.

....

2 Which coil has more turns in a step-down transformer?

....

Practice

3 Explain why the secondary current is greater than the primary current in a step-down transformer.

....

....

....

Challenge

4 Explain how transformers work. In your answer, consider:

- the physics that allows them to function
- the purpose of the step-up transformer
- why we need step-down transformers.

....

....

....

....

....

....

5 Imagine that a conducting material was created that had zero resistance at normal working temperatures. State how this would affect the use of the devices you have studied in this chapter if this material was used to make the power lines and wires carrying current around the country. Explain your answer.

....

....

....

....

....

....

PEER ASSESSMENT

Swap your answer with a partner and compare your ideas. Which ideas have you both thought of? Are there any ideas that your partner thought of, but that you did not?

Having seen your partner's answer, how would you improve your own answer?

> Chapter 22

The nuclear atom

> Atomic structure

Exercise 22.1

IN THIS EXERCISE YOU WILL:

check your understanding of the structure of the atom.

Focus

1   Figure 22.1 shows a simple model of an atom.

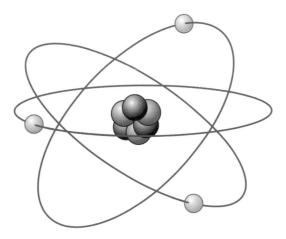

Figure 22.1: A simple model of an atom.

a   Label the nucleus and an electron on Figure 22.1.

b   State which part of the atom contains most of its mass. ....

c   State which part of the atom contains all of its positive charge. ....

Practice

2   Explain the following statements, in terms of electron movement.

   a   When sodium (symbol Na) becomes ionised, it becomes Na⁺.

   ....

   b   When oxygen (symbol O) becomes ionised, it becomes O^{2-}.

   ....

Challenge

3   A physicist decided to make a new element by firing protons at a uranium atom, in an attempt to get them to be absorbed by the nucleus. The experiment was successful and the new particle had an overall charge of +3, whilst the number of nucleons increased by two.

   a   Describe how the new particle could become neutral.

   ....

   b   State how the structure of the nucleus has changed.

   ....

Exercise 22.2

IN THIS EXERCISE YOU WILL:

> check your understanding of the alpha-scattering experiment and how it changed science.

TIP

It is important to know how our understanding of atomic structure progressed. It is a good example of how science progresses. It is worthwhile to first look at the Greek idea and how they came to it, leading to the Thomson ('plum pudding') model, which was followed by the nuclear model. The reasons why the nuclear experiment disproved the Thomson model are important. It is also worth realising that the nuclear model was also modified by Niels Bohr.

Focus

1   The alpha-scattering experiment used alpha radiation to investigate atoms in a thin sheet of gold foil.

   Cross out the **incorrect** words in the following sentences.

   a   Alpha particles have a positive / negative charge.

   b   An alpha particle is bigger / smaller than a gold atom.

   c   The nucleus of a gold atom has a positive / negative charge.

Practice

2 Figure 22.2 shows the paths of some alpha particles as they approached the nucleus of a gold atom.

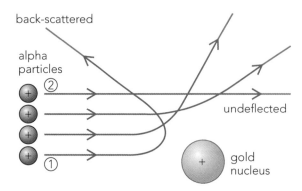

Figure 22.2: Paths of alpha particles as they approached a gold nucleus.

a Explain what it means to say that an alpha particle was 'back-scattered'.

....

....

....

....

b Explain why the alpha particle labelled was back-scattered.

....

....

....

....

c Explain why the alpha particle labelled is described as undeflected.

....

....

....

d Explain why this alpha particle was undeflected as it passed the gold nucleus.

....

....

....

....

e   Many of the alpha particles were deflected through a range of angles. State the conclusion
     that was drawn from this observation.

     ....

Challenge

3   Explain how the alpha-scattering experiment changed the understanding of the atom.

     ....

     ....

     ....

     ....

› Protons, neutrons and electrons

KEY WORDS

proton number (Z): the number of protons in an atomic nucleus

nucleon number (A): the number of protons and neutrons in an atomic nucleus

neutron number (N): the number of neutrons in the nucleus of an atom

neutron: an electrically neutral particle found in the atomic nucleus

isotope: isotopes of an element have the same proton number but different nucleon numbers

nuclide: a 'species' of nucleus having particular values of proton number and nucleon number

KEY EQUATION

proton number + neutron number = nucleon number

$Z + N = A$

Exercise 22.3

IN THIS EXERCISE YOU WILL:

practise using the notation we use to represent a nucleus.

Focus

1   Name the particles that make up the nucleus of sodium.

....

....

Practice

2   A particular atom of carbon (C) is represented like this:

$^{13}_{6}C$

a   State the value of its proton number Z. ....

b   State the value of its nucleon number A. ....

c   Calculate the value of its neutron number N.

....

3   A particular atom of oxygen (O) is made up of eight protons and eight neutrons.

In the space below, write the symbol for this nucleus in the form $^{A}_{Z}O$.

Challenge

4   Complete the table by identifying the subatomic particles described.

Description	Which particles?
These particles make up the nucleus [there are two answers].	
These particles orbit the nucleus.	
These particles have very little mass.	
These particles have no electric charge.	
The charge on these particles is equal and opposite to the charge on an electron.	

Exercise 22.4

IN THIS EXERCISE YOU WILL:

check your recall and understanding of isotopes and use your knowledge to identify some elements in the periodic table.

Focus

1   a   State what is the same for two isotopes of an element.

....

b   State what is different for two isotopes of an element.

....

Practice

2   Figure 22.3 represents an atom of an isotope of boron (B).

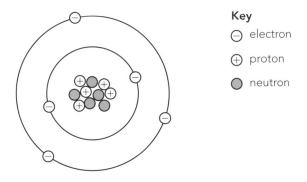

Key

⊖   electron

⊕   proton

⬤   neutron

Figure 22.3: The structure of an atom of an isotope of boron.

Write down the symbol for this nuclide in the form $_{Z}^{A}X$.

....

Challenge

3   The table shows some values of Z, N and A for six different nuclides.

Complete the table as follows:

- Fill in the missing values of Z, N and A, in the second, third and fourth columns.
- Use the Periodic Table to identify the elements, and write your answer in the fifth column.
- Finally, in the last column, write the symbol for each nuclide in the form ${}^A_Z X$.

Nuclide	Proton number Z	Neutron number N	Nucleon number A	Name of element	Nuclide symbol ${}^A_Z X$
Nu-1	4	5			
Nu-2	5	7			
Nu-3		4	8		
Nu-4	6		11		
Nu-5		6	11		

Exercise 22.5

IN THIS EXERCISE YOU WILL:

> check your understanding of the connection between proton and nucleon number and the physical properties of the nucleus

> practise balancing a simple nuclear equation, using the conservation of mass and charge.

TIP

The key to balancing nuclear equations is to realise that some things have to be the same on both sides:

- mass

- charge

Focus

1 $^{235}_{92}\text{U}$ is the symbol for uranium.

State the mass of a uranium nucleus.

....

Practice

2   State the charge on a uranium-235 nucleus.

....

3   This nucleus loses a neutron. State the new notation for this nucleus.

....

Challenge

4   Write a balanced nuclear equation for the event described in Question **3**.

....

PEER ASSESSMENT

Make a mind map to summarise the key facts in this chapter. Once you have made it, swap it with someone else and review each other's work. Can you make any improvements to your mind map?

Chapter 23

Radioactivity

> Radioactivity all around us

KEY WORDS

radiation: energy spreading out from a source carried by particles or waves

alpha particle (α-particle): a particle of two protons and two neutrons emitted by an atomic nucleus during radioactive decay

beta particle (β-particle): An electron emitted by a nucleus during radioactive decay

gamma ray (γ-ray): electromagnetic radiation emitted by an atomic nucleus during radioactive decay

radioactive substance: a substance that decays by emitting radiation from its atomic nuclei

penetration: how far radiation can travel into different materials

ionising radiation: radiation, for example from radioactive substances, that causes ionisation

count rate: the number of nuclear disintegrations per second. Measured in counts/min or counts/s

background radiation: the nuclear radiation from the environment to which we are exposed all the time, due to the disintegration of unstable nuclei

---

Exercise 23.1

IN THIS EXERCISE YOU WILL:

practise describing the ways in which an unstable nucleus decays.

TIP

The properties and the natures of the three types of radiation are very clearly connected and seeing that connection helps in remembering them.

An alpha particle is VERY large and heavy, and is about 8000 times the mass of a beta particle. Because it is large, it has a lot of collisions with the material it is passing through, and is therefore easily stopped and has a short range in air. Because it has a lot of mass, it does a lot of damage when it collides with atoms – it's very ionising. Gamma is electromagnetic radiation. It has no intrinsic mass and no charge, so it does not interact with matter as much as alpha or beta. This means it has a VERY large range in air and is difficult to stop. It also means that it isn't very ionising.

Focus

1 Figure 23.1 shows how the three types of radiation from radioactive substances are absorbed by different materials.

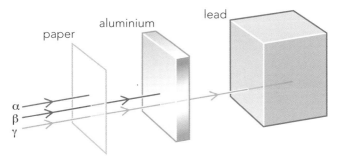

Figure 23.1: A comparison of how the three types of radiation are absorbed by different materials.

a Figure 23.1 uses symbols. Write the full names of those symbols.

i α ....

ii β ....

iii γ ....

b State which type of radiation is the most penetrating. ....

c State which type of radiation can be absorbed by a few centimetres of air or by a thin sheet

of paper. ....

d State which types of radiation are absorbed by a thick sheet of lead. ....

2 The radiation from radioactive substances is called 'ionising radiation'. This is because it can damage atoms, causing them to become ions.

Explain the meaning of the term 'ion'.

....

....

3 a State which type of ionising radiation has no mass. ....

b State which type of ionising radiation has a positive charge. ....

c State which type of ionising radiation is an electron. ....

d State which type of ionising radiation is the same as a helium nucleus. ....

e State which type of ionising radiation travels at the speed of light. ....

f State which type of ionising radiation has a negative charge. ....

g State which type of ionising radiation is a form of electromagnetic radiation.

....

4 What property of nuclear radiation is used to detect it?

....

Practice

5 Explain what causes nuclear instability.

....

....

6 Geiger counters, film badges and spark counters are all used to detect nuclear radiation. What do they all have in common, in the way they perform their function?

....

....

....

Challenge

7 Figure 23.2 shows the count rate measured after each of the barriers shown. The source is on the left.

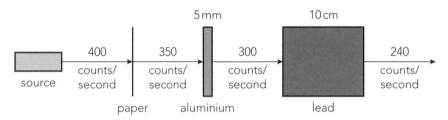

Figure 23.2: A diagram showing changing count rates through various materials.

a State how many alpha particles were emitted per second.

....

b State the background count.

....

8   Describe how you could use an electric field to tell whether a source was emitting one, two or three types of radiation in a narrow beam of radiation.

....

....

....

....

....

....

....

....

....

....

TIP

Only charged particles are affected by electric fields and only moving charged particles are affected by magnetic fields. Opposite charges move in opposite directions in the same field.

9   Considering the kinetic energy and the charge of each, explain the ionising ability of the three types of nuclear radiation.

....

....

....

> The microscopic picture

KEY WORDS

radioactive decay: the disintegration of the nucleus of radioactive substance when its nuclei emit radiation

alpha decay: the decay of a radioactive nucleus by emission of an alpha particle. The general equation for this decay is $^{A}_{Z}X = ^{A-4}_{Z-2}Y + ^{4}_{2}\alpha$

beta decay: the decay of a radioactive nucleus by emission of a beta particle

Exercise 23.2

IN THIS EXERCISE YOU WILL:

> practise writing and interpreting nuclear equations.

Focus

1   There are two types of particle that can be emitted during radioactive decay, alpha and beta.
    The table shows the symbols used for these particles when we write decay equations.

Particle	Symbol	Composition
alpha, α	$^{4}_{2}\text{He}$	
beta, β	$^{0}_{-1}\text{e}$	

In the last column of the table, state the composition of each of them in terms of the subatomic particles: protons, neutrons and electrons.

2   The equation shows how an isotope of radium decays to become an isotope of radon.

$$^{223}_{88}\text{Ra} \rightarrow {}^{219}_{86}\text{Rn} + {}^{4}_{2}\text{He} + \text{energy}$$

a   State the chemical symbol for radium. ....

b   State the chemical symbol for radon. ....

c   State the type of particle that is emitted. ....

We can check that the equation is balanced by counting the number of nucleons before and after the decay, and the number of protons before and after.

For the nucleons, we have $223 = 219 + 4$

d   Show that the number of protons is the same before and after the decay.

    ....

3   a   State which type of radioactive emission does not change the number of protons or

        neutrons in the nucleus. ....

    b   State the type of radioactive emission in which the number of protons in the nucleus
        changes. Also state whether it increases or decreases.

        ....

Practice

4   The equation shows how an isotope of carbon decays to become an isotope of nitrogen.

$$^{15}_{6}\text{C} \rightarrow {}^{15}_{7}\text{N} + {}^{0}_{-1}\text{e} + \text{energy}$$

Show that this equation is balanced.

....

5   Complete the following decay equation, which shows how an isotope of polonium decays to become an isotope of lead:

$^{211}_{84}\text{Po} \rightarrow {}^{207}_{82}\text{Pb} + $ .... $ + $ ....

6   An isotope of protactinium (symbol Pa) has 91 protons and 140 neutrons in its nucleus.

   a   Write the symbol for this nuclide. ....

   The nuclide decays by alpha decay to become an isotope of actinium (symbol Ac).

   b   Write a complete decay equation for this decay.

   ....

Challenge

7   $^{238}_{92}\text{U}$ decays by alpha decay, then beta decay, then beta decay. Deduce the atomic and mass numbers of the daughter nucleus after the third decay and state the element it has become.

....

....

....

....

〉 Radioactive decay

KEY WORDS

random process: a process that happens at a random rate rather than at a steady rate; in radioactive decay, it is impossible to predict which atom will be the next to decay, or when a given atom will decay

half-life: the average time taken for half the atoms in a sample of a radioactive material to decay

Exercise 23.3

IN THIS EXERCISE YOU WILL:

check your understanding of half-life.

Focus

1 A sample of a radioactive substance contains 2400 undecayed atoms.

   a Calculate the number of atoms that will remain after three half-lives.

   ....

   ....

   ....

   b Calculate the number of atoms that will decay during three half-lives.

   ....

   ....

   ....

   c Explain why these calculations are not likely to match actual measurements.

   ....

   ....

Practice

2 A Physicist was conducting some experiments using radioactive sources. Having finished, she locked the sources in a lead lined room and left work at 5.00 p.m. She returned at 9.00 a.m. the following morning and realised that she had not turned off the Geiger-Müller tube and scaler she had been using. The scaler showed a value of 172 800. Assume that the counter had been at zero when she left.

   a State the background count. ....

   b Calculate the background count rate per second.

   ....

Challenge

3 Some data for an experiment is shown in Table 23.1.

	1: No source	2: With only source	3: Paper between source and detector	4: 3 mm thick aluminium sheet between source and detector	5: 20 cm thick lead block between source and detector
Count rate / counts/min	45	745	622	600	45

Table 23.1: Experimental data.

Explain what you can conclude from the difference in readings between the columns.

....

....

....

....

Exercise 23.4

IN THIS EXERCISE YOU WILL:

> describe different types of radioactive decay

> practise determining the half-life of different radioactive samples.

Focus

1 State what radioactive decay is.

....

Practice

2 Describe radioactive decay. In your description, include:

- the types of decay
- their effect on the parent nucleus
- nuclear equations, as appropriate.

....

....

....

....

....

3 A sample of a radioactive substance contains 1000 undecayed atoms. Its half-life is 4.5 years.

Calculate the number that will remain undecayed after 9 years.

....

....

4 A radioactive substance has a half-life of 13 years.

Calculate the time it will take for the number of undecayed atoms in a sample to fall to one-eighth of their original number.

....

....

5 Table 23.2 shows how the activity of a radioactive sample changed as it decayed.

Time / h	0	2	4	6	8
Activity / counts per second	500	280	160	95	55

Table 23.2: Radioactive decay.

On the grid, draw a graph of activity against time and use it to deduce the half-life of the substance.

Show your method on the graph.

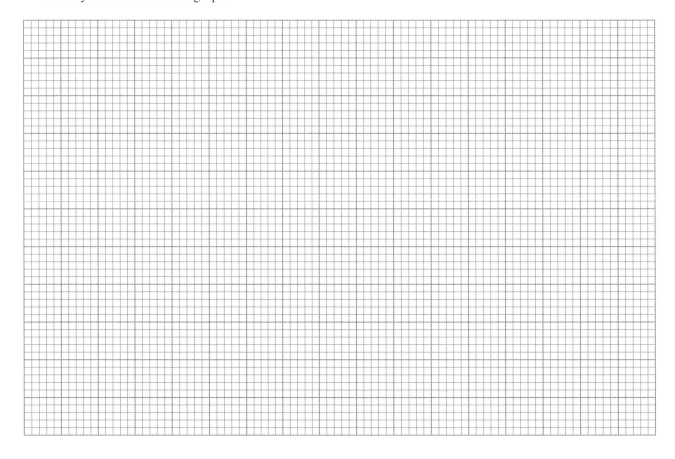

The half-life is approximately ....

6   Figure 23.3 shows counts per minute in a sample of a radioactive substance as it decayed. When the material had decayed to a very low level, the detector still recorded background radiation.

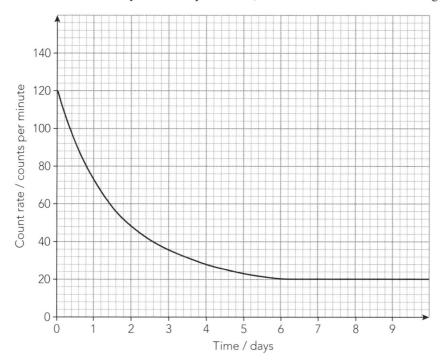

Figure 23.3: A graph of count rate against time for a radioactive sample.

a   From the graph, determine the background count rate. ....

b   Determine the initial count rate due to the radioactive substance by calculating:

initial count rate − background count rate ....

c   Determine the approximate half-life of the substance.

There are **two** different ways to do this. Find both. Show your working on the graph and in the space provided.

The half-life is approximately ....

Challenge

7   A source contains two different elements with unstable nuclei. Isotope A has a half-life of 16 hours, isotope B has a half-life of 8 hours. The count rate from each is 128 per second to begin with. Calculate the count rate after 32 hours.

   ....

   ....

   ....

   ....

> Using radioisotopes

KEY WORDS

radioisotope: a radioactive isotope of an element

radioactive tracing: a technique that uses a radioactive substance to trace the flow of liquid or gas, or to find the position of cancerous tissue in the body

Exercise 23.5

IN THIS EXERCISE YOU WILL:

> practise your understanding of the applications of radioisotopes in the real world.

Focus

1   The first column of the table shows some uses of radioactive substances.

   In the second column, write the appropriate code letter or letters from the list below:

   A   Some radiation is very penetrating.

   B   Some radiation is readily absorbed.

   C   Ionising radiation damages cells.

   D   Radiation is easily detected.

   E   Radioactive substances decay at a known rate.

Use of radioactivity	Code letter(s)
finding the age of an ancient object	
diagnosing cancer and destroying cancerous tissue	
sterilising medical equipment	
controlling the thickness of paper in a paper mill	
detecting smoke in the air	
tracing leaks from underground pipes	
irradiating food	

> **TIP**
>
> It is important to grasp the difference between contaminated and irradiated. Soft fruit is often irradiated to give it a longer shelf life. It is safe to eat. Ionising radiation has passed through it, killing bacteria. Contamination is very different. If the fruit was contaminated, it would have a source of ionising radiation in it or on it. Eating this could be very dangerous indeed, as the source would then be inside you, ionising living tissue.

Practice

2   List and explain the precautions that can be taken to reduce the danger to living things from ionising radiation.

   ....

   ....

   ....

Challenge

3   From Table 23.3 on the following page, choose the most appropriate source for each of these applications. Explain your choice in each case.

   a   A medical tracer.

   ....

   ....

   b   To check the thickness of paper in a mill.

   ....

   ....

c In a domestic smoke detector.

....

....

d To treat cancer by radiotherapy.

....

....

Radioisotope	Emits	Half-life
Tc-99	gamma	6 hours
Ba-133	gamma	10.5 years
Kr-85	beta, gamma	10.8 years
Am-241	alpha, gamma	432 years
Cf-252	alpha, gamma	2.6 years
La-140	beta, gamma	40.2 hours
U-234	alpha, gamma	250 000 years
I-129	beta, gamma	1 600 000 years

Table 23.3: Radioactive decay and half-life of some isotopes.

PEER ASSESSMENT

Make a set of flash cards or a mind map to summarise the key facts in this chapter.

Once you have made a set or cards or your mind map, swap this with someone else and review each other's work.

Having reviewed your partner's work, how can you improve your own work?

Chapter 24

Earth and the Solar System

> The Earth

KEY WORDS

axis: an imaginary line through the poles, around which a planet spins

cyclical: Something that is cyclical has a regular period; for example, the Earth's rotation on its axis and its rotation around the Sun are both cyclical: 24 hours and 365 days respectively

orbital: the path taken by an orbiting object; also refers to the fact that an object is in orbit

---

KEY EQUATION

Average orbital speed = $2 \times \pi \times$ average radius of orbit / time

$$v = \frac{2\pi r}{T}$$

Exercise 24.1

IN THIS EXERCISE YOU WILL:

recall key facts about the Earth and the Moon.

Focus

1   The Earth's rotation on its axis and also its rotation around the Sun are cyclical and periodic. State how long the Earth takes to:

   a   rotate once on its axis.

   ....

   b   orbit the Sun once.

   ....

Practice

2   Explain the observations that lead us to the conclusion that the Earth spins on its axis.

   ....

   ....

   ....

Challenge

3 Explain the phases of the Moon.

....

....

....

4 The Earth orbits the Sun at an average distance of 1.5×10^8 km and the period of orbit is 365 days. Calculate the average orbital speed of the Earth around the Sun.

....

....

....

> The Solar System

Figure 24.1: The Solar System.

> KEY WORDS
>
> **gaseous:** made of gases
>
> **elliptical:** in the shape of an ellipse; an ellipse looks like a circle that has been squashed from left and right, or from top and bottom
>
> **density:** the mass of 1 cm³ or 1 m³ of a substance
>
> **nuclear fusion:** the combination of light nuclei to make a heavier nucleus, releasing energy; this is how stars produce electromagnetic radiation

Exercise 24.2

IN THIS EXERCISE YOU WILL:

check your understanding of the Solar System.

Focus

1   Fill in the blanks in the paragraph below.

There are three celestial bodies that orbit the Sun. These are ....,

.... and .... Moons orbit ....

2   What shape is the orbit of the Mars, as shown in Figure 24.2?

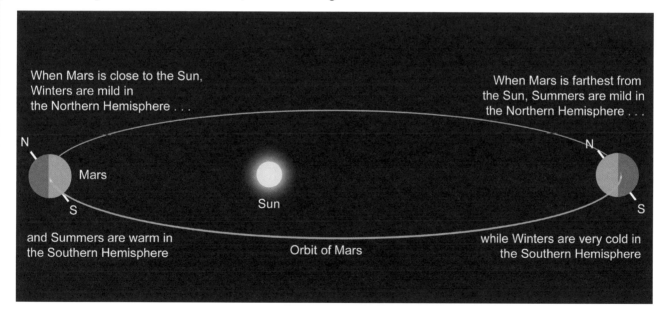

Figure 24.2: The orbit of Mars around the Sun.

....

Practice

3 List the rocky planets that orbit the Sun.

....

4

	Mercury	Venus	Earth	Mars	Jupiter	Saturn	Uranus	Neptune
Diameter / km	4879	12 104	12 756	6792	142 984	120 536	51 118	2370
Mass / 10^{24} kg	0.330	4.87	5.97	0.642	1898	568	86.8	0.0146
Gravity / m/s^2	3.7	8.9	9.8	3.7	23.1	9.0	8.7	0.7
Average distance from Sun / 10^6 km	57.9	108.2	149.6	227.9	778.6	1433.5	2872.5	5906.4
Orbital period / days	88.0	224.7	365.2	687.0	4331	10 747	30 589	90 560
Mean temperature / °C	167	464	15	−65	−110	−140	−195	−225

a A learner looking at the data above concludes that 'The larger the planet, the bigger the gravity will be on the surface'. Discuss whether this is a valid conclusion. Use the data from the table to support your argument.

....

....

....

b Suggest a reason why the surface temperature of Venus is higher than that of Mercury, despite the fact that Mercury is closer to the Sun. Use the data to support your conclusion.

....

....

....

Challenge

5 Explain how the Solar System formed and how it led to some planets being rocky and others being gaseous.

....

....

....

....

6 **a** Explain why the distances from the Sun are quoted as average.

....

....

....

   b Use this idea to comment on how the speed of orbit might change during each planet's year. Explain this, using ideas about the Sun's gravity.

....

....

....

   c Using the law of conservation of energy, explain the why the speeds must change in this way.

....

....

....

> Chapter 25

Stars and the Universe

KEY WORDS

redshift: the apparent increase in wavelength of electromagnetic radiation emitted from a distant star

light-year: the distance travelled by light in one year

KEY EQUATIONS

1 light-year = 9.5×10^{15} m

speed at which a galaxy is moving away from Earth = Hubble constant × distance from the Earth

$v = H_0 d$

TIP

All stars start life the same way. It's what happens after the stable phase that depends on mass. More mass means more extreme events and conclusions – supernovae leading to neutron stars and black holes. The more massive the star, the bigger the forces acting inside it, so the more dense the core will be. This is why the biggest stars end up as black holes – so dense that even light can't escape the pull of their gravity.

Exercise 25.1

IN THIS EXERCISE YOU WILL:

- check your understanding of the scale and origin of the universe
- describe and explain 'redshift'.

Figure 25.1: The Milky Way.

Focus

1   Figure 25.1 shows the Milky Way. State what the Milky Way is.

....

2   State what a light-year is.

....

Practice

3   Explain the term 'redshift'.

....

....

> **TIP**
>
> It is a common mistake to think that red- or blueshift refers to light changing colour. It isn't. It is a reference to the way wavelength changes in the visible spectrum. If you move from blue to red, the wavelength gets longer; from red to blue, it gets shorter. If you have redshifted microwaves, they might move into the radio range, or blueshifted might end up with infrared wavelength.

Challenge

4 Canis Major Dwarf is the nearest galaxy to ours. Describe and explain the challenge that we face in getting there.

....

....

....

Exercise 25.2

KEY EQUATION

$$\frac{d}{v} = \frac{1}{H_0}$$

IN THIS EXERCISE YOU WILL:

> practise calculations to determine the scale and age of the universe.

Focus

1 State how far one light-year is in metres.

....

2 a State Hubble's equation.

....

b State the accepted value of Hubble's constant H_0.

....

3 Define cosmic microwave background radiation.

....

4 Explain what cosmic microwave background radiation suggests to us about the universe.

....

Practice

5   Proxima Centauri is 4.03×10^{13} km away from Earth. Calculate how far this is in light-years.

....

....

....

....

6   Explain how we know the values of v (recessional velocity) and d (the distance to a galaxy).

....

....

Challenge

7   Explain how Hubble's equation allows us to calculate an age for the universe.

....

....

....

8   Explain how Hubble's equation supports the Big Bang Theory.

....

....

Figure 25.2: A supernova.

9 Figure 25.2 shows a supernova explosion. Describe the life cycle of a star. Consider two different stars: one the size of the Sun and another which will undergo a supernova. State the condition that dictates a supernova and what is produced in a supernova.

....

....

....

....

....

....

....

....

....

....

....

....

....

10 Write a letter to a younger sibling to explain why we have seasons and day and night.
You should include a scientific explanation of how the Sun began and why the Moon has phases.

....

....

....

....

....

....

....

....

....

....

....

....

....

....

....

PEER ASSESSMENT

Once you are finished, you can assess your work against the table below.
Draw a smiley face per point correctly made in each section. Revisit any areas that you found difficult.

Section	Correct comments
Day and night	
Seasons	
Phases of the Moon	
Origin of the Sun	

> Glossary

Key Words

a.c. generator: a device, such as a dynamo, used to generate alternating current (a.c.)

absolute (kelvin) scale of temperature (K): the zero of the kelvin scale is absolute zero, the temperature at which all atomic vibration in a solid stops; it is −273 °C

acceleration: the rate of change of an object's velocity

air resistance: the force on a moving object because it is colliding with air molecules as it moves

alpha decay: the decay of a radioactive nucleus by emission of an alpha particle. The general equation for this decay is $_Z^A X = _{Z-2}^{A-4} Y + _2^4 \alpha$

alpha particle (α-particle): a particle of two protons and two neutrons emitted by an atomic nucleus during radioactive decay

alternating current (a.c.): electric current that flows first one way, then the other, in a circuit

amp, ampere (A): the SI unit of electric current

amplitude: the greatest height of a wave above its undisturbed level

angle of incidence: the angle between the incident ray and the normal

angle of reflection: the angle between the reflected ray and the normal

angle of refraction: the angle between the refracted ray and the normal

axis: an imaginary line through the poles, around which a planet spins

background radiation: the nuclear radiation from the environment to which we are exposed all the time, due to the disintegration of unstable nuclei

battery: two or more electrical cells connected together in series; the word may also be used to mean a single cell

battery capacity: a measure of the stored energy. Measured in Ah ('amp-hours')

beta decay: the decay of a radioactive nucleus by emission of a beta particle

beta particle (β-particle): an electron emitted by a nucleus during radioactive decay

biomass fuel: a material, recently living, used as a fuel

Brownian motion: the motion of small particles suspended in a liquid or gas, caused by molecular bombardment

cell: a device that provides a potential difference in a circuit

centre of gravity: the point at which the mass of an object can be considered to be concentrated

chemical energy: energy stored in chemical substances and which can be released in a chemical reaction

commutator: a device used to allow current to flow to and from the coil of a d.c. motor or generator

compression: a region of a sound wave where the particles are pushed close together

conduction: the transfer of thermal energy or electricity through a material without the material itself moving

conductor: (1) a substance that allows an electric current to pass through it; (2) a substance that transmits thermal energy

convection: the transfer of thermal energy through a material by movement of the material itself

converging lens: rays entering the lens parallel to the principal axis pass through the principal focus after leaving the lens; these lenses usually form real images

coulomb (C): the SI unit of electric charge; $1 \text{ C} = 1 \text{ A s}$ ('1 amp-second')

count rate: the number of nuclear disintegrations per second. Measured in counts/min or counts/s

critical angle: the minimum angle of incidence at which total internal reflection occurs; it has the symbol c

current: a flow of electric charge

current: the charge passing a point in a circuit per unit time

current–voltage characteristic: a graph showing how the current in a component depends on the p.d. across it

cyclical: Something that is cyclical has a regular period; for example, the Earth's rotation on its axis and its rotation around the Sun are both cyclical: 24 hours and 365 days respectively

deceleration: negative acceleration (that is to say, the rate of decrease of velocity)

density: (1) the ratio of mass to volume for a substance; (2) the mass of 1 cm^3 or 1 m^3 of a substance

diffraction: when a wave spreads out as it travels through a gap or past the edge of an object

diode: an electrical component that allows electric current to flow in one direction only

direct current (d.c.): electric current that flows in the same direction all the time

diverging lens: rays entering the lens parallel to the principal axis, diverge as if they came from the principal focus; these lenses form virtual images. Diverge means to get further apart

doing work: transferring energy

efficiency: the fraction of energy that is transferred to a useful form

electric field: a region where charged objects experience force; the direction of the field at a point in the field is the direction of force on positive charge

electromagnet: (1) a coil of wire that becomes a magnet when a current flows in it; (2) when current is passed through a solenoid, it becomes a magnet; this kind of magnet can be turned on and off and the strength can be controlled by the size of the current flowing through the solenoid

electromagnetic induction: the process by which a potential difference is induced across a conductor when the magnetic field around it changes

electromagnetic radiation: energy travelling in the form of waves

electromagnetic spectrum: the family of radiations similar to light

electromotive force (e.m.f): the electrical work done in moving +1 C around a complete circuit

electron: a negatively charged particle, smaller than an atom

electrostatic charge: a property of an object that causes it to attract or repel other objects with charge

elliptical: in the shape of an ellipse; an ellipse looks like a circle that has been squashed from left and right, or from top and bottom

energy: the capacity to do work

equilibrium: when no net force and no net moment act on a body

extension: the total increase in length of a spring when a load is attached

Fleming's left-hand rule: a rule that gives the relationship between the directions of force, field and current when a current flows across a magnetic field

Fleming's right-hand rule: a rule that gives the relationship between the directions of force, field and current when a current is induced by moving a conductor relative to a magnetic field

focal length: the distance between the centre of the lens and the principal focus

force: the action of one body on a second body that causes its velocity to change

fossil fuel: a material, formed from long-dead material, used as a fuel

frequency: the number of vibrations per second or waves per second passing a point

fuse: a device used to prevent excessive currents flowing in a circuit

gamma ray (γ-ray): electromagnetic radiation emitted by an atomic nucleus during radioactive decay

gaseous: made of gases

geothermal: the energy stored in hot rocks underground

gravitational potential energy: the energy stored in an object that is raised up against the force of gravity

half-life: the average time taken for half the atoms in a sample of a radioactive material to decay

hard magnetic material: a material that, once magnetised, is difficult to demagnetise, e.g. steel

impulse of a force: the product of a force and the time for which it acts (impulse = Ft)

infrared radiation: electromagnetic radiation whose wavelength is greater than that of visible light; sometimes known as heat radiation

insulator: (1) a substance that does not conduct electricity; (2) a substance that transmits thermal energy very poorly

internal energy: the energy of an object; the total kinetic and potential energies of its particles

ionising radiation: radiation, for example from radioactive substances, that causes ionisation

isotope: isotopes of an element have the same proton number but different nucleon numbers

joule (J): the SI unit of work or energy

kinetic energy (k.e.): the energy stored in a moving object

light-dependent resistor (LDR): a device whose resistance decreases when light shines on it

light-emitting diode (LED): a type of diode that emits light when a current flows through it

light-year: the distance travelled by light in one year

limit of proportionality: the point beyond which the extension of an object is no longer proportional to the load producing it

load: a force that causes a spring to extend

longitudinal wave: a wave in which the vibration is forward and back, along the direction in which the wave is travelling

magnet: a device which exerts a force on magnetic materials

magnetic field: the region of space around a magnet or electric current in which a magnet will feel a force

magnetic field line: the direction of a magnetic field line at a point in the magnetic field is the direction of the force on a North pole placed at that point

magnetic material: common magnetic materials are iron, steel, nickel, cobalt

magnetisation: causing a piece of material to be magnetised; a material is magnetised when it produces a magnetic field around itself

mass: a measure of the quantity of matter in an object at rest relative to the observer

molecular model of matter: a model in which matter consists of molecules in motion

moment of a force: the turning effect of a force about a point

momentum: the product of an object's mass and its velocity (momentum $p = mv$)

negative charge: one of the two types of electric charge, the other is positive charge

neutral: having no overall positive or negative electric charge

neutron: an electrically neutral particle found in the atomic nucleus

neutron number (N): the number of neutrons in the nucleus of an atom

non-renewable: energy resource which, once used, is gone forever

normal: means 'at 90° to'; a normal is a line at 90° to a surface (for example, the surface of a mirror) or boundary between two materials (for example, the boundary between air and glass)

nuclear energy: energy stored in the nucleus of an atom

nuclear fission: the process by which energy is released by the splitting of a large heavy nucleus into two or more lighter nuclei

nuclear fusion: the process by which energy is released by the joining together of two small light nuclei to form a new heavier nucleus; this is how stars produce electromagnetic radiation

nucleon number (A): the number of protons and neutrons in an atomic nucleus

nucleon: a particle found in the atomic nucleus: a proton or a neutron

nuclide: a 'species' of nucleus having particular values of proton number and nucleon number

ohm (Ω): the SI unit of electrical resistance; $1\,\Omega = 1\,\text{V/A}$ ('1 volt per amp')

ohmic resistor: any conductor for which the current in it is directly proportional to the p.d. across it

orbital: the path taken by an orbiting object; also refers to the fact that an object is in orbit

p.d. (potential difference): another name for the voltage between two points

penetration: how far radiation can travel into different materials

period: the time for one complete oscillation of a pendulum, one complete vibration or the passage of one complete wave

pitch: how high or low a note sounds

plane (mirror): plane means 'flat', so a plane mirror is a flat mirror

positive charge: one of the two types of electric charge, the other is negative charge

potential divider: a part of a circuit used to provide a variable potential difference

potential divider: two resistors connected in series to provide a variable potential difference

power lines: cables used to carry electricity from power stations to consumers

power: the rate at which work is done or energy is transferred

pressure: the force acting per unit area at right angles to a surface

principal axis: the line passing through the centre of a lens, perpendicular to its surface

principal focus: the point at which rays of light parallel to the axis converge after passing through a converging lens

principle of conservation of energy: the total energy of interacting objects is constant provided no net external force acts

principle of conservation of momentum: the total momentum of interacting objects is constant provided no net external force acts

proton: a positively charged particle found in the atomic nucleus

proton number (Z): the number of protons in an atomic nucleus

radiation: energy spreading out from a source carried by particles or waves

radioactive decay: the disintegration of the nucleus of radioactive substance when its nuclei emit radiation

radioactive substance: a substance that decays by emitting radiation from its atomic nuclei

radioactive tracing: a technique that uses a radioactive substance to trace the flow of liquid or gas, or to find the position of cancerous tissue in the body

radioisotope: a radioactive isotope of an element

random process: a process that happens at a random rate rather than at a steady rate; in radioactive decay, it is impossible to predict which atom will be the next to decay, or when a given atom will decay

rarefaction: a region of a sound wave where the particles are further apart

ray diagram: a diagram showing the paths of typical rays of light

real image: an image that can be formed on a screen

redshift: the apparent increase in wavelength of electromagnetic radiation emitted from a distant star

reflection: the change in direction of a ray of light when it strikes a surface without passing through it

refraction: the bending of a ray of light on passing from one material to another

refractive index: the ratio of the speeds of a wave in two different regions

relay: an electromagnetically operated switch

renewable: energy resource which, when used, will be replenished naturally

resistance: the ratio of the p.d. across a component to the current flowing through it

resistor: a component in an electric circuit which limits or controls the current flowing

resultant force: (1) the change in momentum per unit time;

resultant force: (2) the single force that has the same effect on a body as two or more forces

right-hand grip rule: the rule used to determine the direction of the magnetic field around an electric current (see Fleming's right-hand rule)

Sankey diagram: a diagram to show all the energy transfers taking place in a process using arrows. Each transfer is shown by a separate arrow. The width of the arrows represents the amount of energy being transferred

scalar: a quantity that only has size (examples include speed, time, mass, energy, temperature)

slip rings: a device used to allow current to flow to and from the coil of an a.c. motor or generator

soft magnetic material: a material that, once magnetised, can easily be demagnetised, e.g. soft iron

solenoid: a long narrow coil of wire

specific heat capacity (c): the energy required per kilogram and per degree Celsius to raise the temperature of a substance

spectrum: waves, or colours of light, separated out in order according to their wavelengths

speed: the distance travelled by an object in unit timespeed of light: the speed at which light travels; this is 3.0×10^8 m/s in a vacuum

spring constant: the load required to produce an extension of 1 m in a spring

temperature: a measure of the average kinetic energy of the molecules of a substance

terminal velocity: the maximum velocity attained by a falling object

thermistor: a resistor whose resistance changes a lot over a small temperature range

total internal reflection: when a ray of light strikes the inner surface of a solid material and 100% of the light reflects back inside it

transformer: a device used to change the voltage of an a.c. electricity supply

transverse wave: a wave in which the vibration is at right angles to the direction in which the wave is travelling

trip switch: a safety device that automatically switches off a circuit when the current becomes too high

ultrasound: sound waves whose frequency is so high that they cannot be heard

ultraviolet radiation: electromagnetic radiation whose frequency is higher than that of visible light

uniform gravitational field: a region where the acceleration due to gravity is constant

variable resistor: a resistor whose resistance can be changed, for example by turning a knob

vector: a quantity that has both size and direction (examples include force, velocity and acceleration, momentum and gravitational fields, magnetic and electric fields)

velocity: speed in a given direction

virtual image: an image that cannot be formed on a screen; it is formed when rays of light appear to be spreading out from a point

volt (V): the SI unit of voltage (p.d. or e.m.f.); 1 V = 1 J/C ('1 joule per coulomb')

voltage: the 'push' of a battery or power supply in a circuit

watt (W): the SI unit of power; the power when 1 J of work is done in 1 s; 1 W = 1 J/s

wave equation: the equation linking wave speed, frequency and wavelength

wave speed: the speed at which a wave travels

wavefront: a line joining adjacent points on a wave that are all in step with each other

wavelength: the distance between adjacent crests (or troughs) of a wave

weight: the downward force of gravity that acts on an object because of its mass

work done: the amount of energy transferred

> Acknowledgements

The authors and publishers acknowledge the following sources of copyright material and are grateful for the permissions granted. While every effort has been made, it has not always been possible to identify the sources of all the material used, or to trace all copyright holders. If any omissions are brought to our notice, we will be happy to include the appropriate acknowledgements on reprinting.

Thanks to the following for permission to reproduce images:

Dennis Hallinan/Getty Images; Wong Sze Fei / EyeEm/Getty Images; Avalon_Studio/Getty Images

boxster/Getty Images; Tom Merton/Getty Images; Muhammad Fathi Khalid / EyeEm/Getty Images

Robert Brook/Science Photo Library/Getty Images; Jonathan Kitchen/Getty Images

mikroman6/Getty Images; Mark Garlick/Getty Images; Ron Miller/Stocktrek Images/Getty Images

Mark Garlick/Science Photo Library/Getty Images; Science Photo Library - MEHAU KULYK./ Getty Images